DON'T FORGET TO WRITE!

Don't Forget to Write!

Alfred Howarth

An hilarious yet moving account of war-time life

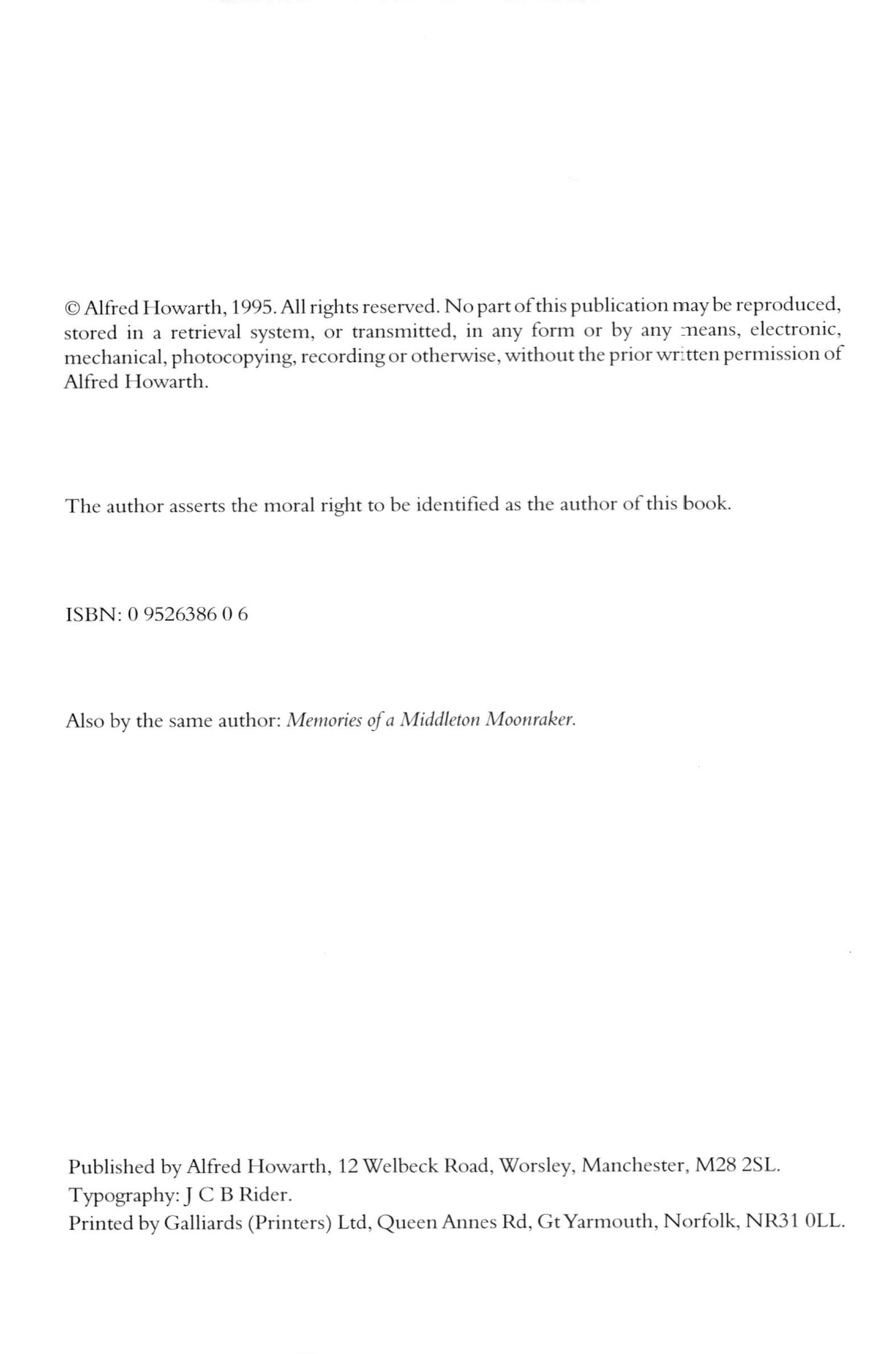

© Alfred Howarth, 1995. All rights reserved. No part of this publication may be reproduced, stored in a retrieval system, or transmitted, in any form or by any means, electronic, mechanical, photocopying, recording or otherwise, without the prior written permission of Alfred Howarth.

The author asserts the moral right to be identified as the author of this book.

ISBN: 0 9526386 0 6

Also by the same author: *Memories of a Middleton Moonraker.*

Published by Alfred Howarth, 12 Welbeck Road, Worsley, Manchester, M28 2SL.
Typography: J C B Rider.
Printed by Galliards (Printers) Ltd, Queen Annes Rd, Gt Yarmouth, Norfolk, NR31 0LL.

Dedication

For Mac, and all the other lads who never made it home.

'... and those who have followed their forebears to Flanders and France, those undefeated in defeat, unalterable in triumph, changing nothing of their ancestors' ways but their weapons.'

T. S. Eliot.

Acknowledgements

I am deeply indebted to my old friend and erstwhile comrade Arthur Walton for the use of what he refers to as his 'Little Black Book'. In this he recorded much of the detail relevant to our peregrinations about the Middle East, so that I was able to bring places and dates into focus.

My thanks are also due to Mrs Barbara Barber, the widow of Eric Barber MBE, who so kindly presented me with a copy of Eric's book *My War*, together with many of her late husband's private papers. I am indeed grateful.

It has also been my good fortune to benefit from enthusiastic advice contributed by another old comrade who served with me in the 71st Searchlight Regiment. Eddie Harrison kindly provided many interesting anecdotes, not to mention several most useful photographs, for all of which I express my warm thanks.

My son Philip contributed a good deal of practical help and encouragement in getting the enterprise off the ground, ably backed up by an equally enthusiastic and knowledgeable Brett Rider. Without their combined expertise I doubt if this record would ever have appeared in print. I offer my sincere thanks to both.

Contents

Early Days	1
Cloud Cuckoo Land	5
Overture & Beginners	8
Curtain Up	14
Breathing Space	20
Red Alert	23
New Pastures	30
Death of the 71st	38
104th LAA Regiment	42
Convoy WS 26	46
Foreign Parts	55
Italy	72
The Sharp End	77
Greece	89
Blighty	109
Last Act	112

Preface

What follows is not in any sense a definitive record of particular World War II military actions or events; such accounts are best left to the experts who, over the years, have provided so much chapter and verse on the various scraps in which British and Commonwealth troops were involved.

Leaving the erudition to the experts then, I have set out my own personal story, starting with the search for a spark of excitement, and which ultimately landed me in the Territorial Army in good time to be caught up in the calamitous events of September 1939.

The account is truthful as far as memory can be trusted but, mindful that some of the characters who roam the pages may not take kindly to having their names bandied about, in whatever context, I have arbitrarily re-christened some of them.

War on any scale is a squalid, hideous business, as those who found themselves in its bloody grip will surely testify. But there were occasions when, amidst all the mayhem, the squaddies' humour surfaced. Often black and desperate humour, yet it had a part to play in our uncertain lives, and I hope I have succeeded, in the following pages, to convey something of the lighter side of those otherwise dismal days.

CHAPTER I

Early Days

There was nothing of particular significance about the 22nd of March 1939, except perhaps that it happened to be my 18th birthday. And as birthdays go it was a dead loss. Adolf Hitler was busy putting the fear of God up most of Europe, making hysterical threats about Danzig and the Czech Sudetenland, and generally putting a noisy damper on celebratory activities of any kind.

But such political shenanigans were esoteric matters quite outside my normal sphere of interest. In those days my political naïvete was chronic. I was more concerned, along with my friend Maurice, to discover what delights and excitement approaching manhood might have in store.

We did not ask for much; simply some means of stepping off the regulating treadmill, however briefly, and having a shot at finding out if life had anything more to offer than the ennui of nine to five (nine to mid-day on Saturdays) and a form of living death on Sundays.

Apart from spiritual pursuits, the Sabbath had nothing to offer lusty young heathens such as we undoubtedly were. Cinemas and dance halls remained dark and silent. Leisure centres, sports complexes and the like were not then even visions of the future.

One aspect of Sunday evenings however did cause a minor *frisson*; a stroll along what Northerners termed the 'Monkey run', where brilliantined, pink faced lads perambulated up and down a predetermined stretch of road, trotting out threadbare, banal one-liners in a brave effort to 'click', *en passant*, with any likely looking girls with an eye for a bright lad. It was to some extent a stimulating exercise, although hardly likely to bring on a cardiac arrest, unless one was fortunate enough to effect a steamy dalliance behind the parochial hall.

We may have cast about for other, more intoxicating pursuits with which to occupy our young restless minds, but we certainly could not afford to spend the shining hours, or the money, on such things as tins of glue. And *coke* was something we burned when coal was unaffordable. *Pot* was a cooking vessel, and *smack* was what one was likely to get for giving cheek!

Our wanderings often took Maurice and me past Thorley Street, now sealed off, and adjoining buildings taken over by a recently formed Territorial

Army unit, the 71st Searchlight Regiment, Royal Artillery. We had paused, on occasion, to observe the purposeful activity of many khaki clad figures on the other side of the barriers. We were intrigued. This was something quite outside our ken, but we were quick to spot one obvious advantage the soldiery enjoyed.

It seemed that on drill nights, a bevy of personable local girls congregated outside the barracks to engage the troops in jolly conversation and *badinage*. I suppose that in to-day's jargon they might be termed 'groupies', but whatever term may have been current in those days, Maurice and I felt that this set up was more or less what we had been vaguely casting about for. If we could get in amongst that macho lot, life would surely take on an entirely new dimension.

The prospect of joining up became more appealing the more we thought about it. Not least of the attractions were the two weeks annual camp, during which period many understanding employers undertook to continue paying at least part wages for any employee absent on TA duties.

There would of course be Army pay. Chatting up the groupies would be something of a bonus.

Rates of pay for Territorials attending camp were:

Gunner	*2/- per day*	*Sergeant*	*6/- per day*
Lance Bombardier	3/3 "	*Staff Sergeant*	8/- "
Bombardier	4/- "	*BQMS*	8/- "
Lance Sergeant	4/9 "	*Battery S/Major*	8/6 "

In addition to all this munificence there was an annual bonus of £3 to £5.

Setting aside some initial qualms, we decided to give it a go and present our eager selves at the barracks on the next drill night.

But now, a minor impediment presented itself; the requirement for signed parental consent. In those days of course, one did not achieve one's majority until the 21st birthday. The problem gave rise to some acrimonious discussion at home. Father was all for it. Said it would make a man of me, whatever he meant by that. Mother, no different from millions of mothers before her, came over all protective, dismissing what she called my 'messing about with guns' as youthful foolhardiness. She gave up the unequal struggle finally, but not without some portentous reminders of mud filled trenches, and other harrowing details from the First World War.

Armed eventually with the required consents, and in something of a sweat, we presented ourselves at the barracks. Already the groupies were

EARLY DAYS

The Barracks, Thorley Street

foregathering in Thorley Street, giggling at each other and patting their hair as if Vidal Sassoon had just finished with it. Maurice fixed his black, furtive eyes upon a tall girl with a chest like a relief map of the Himalayas. 'We're going in to join up!' he announced. Presumably he was just marking her card for when he got his uniform. She gave him a frosty look. 'Oh, good for you shorty' she murmured, and turned away to examine her reflection in a shop window. I grabbed his arm. 'Come on,' I croaked, 'let's go in and get it over with.'

The barracks reeked of new khaki, leather and blanco, a combination of odours I soon came to know well.

The moment we crossed the threshold a soldierly figure of great height confronted us. I was a fraction under six feet, but the khaki clad figure, *en grande tenue*, now eyeing us sharply, could have given me another foot or so. Slim as a lamp post, wearing immaculate boots and spurs, he shone like all the military virtues I was to hear all about later. 'You lads come to join up have you?' he barked over our heads. And without waiting for an answer,'That's the spirit — come on then, follow me.' I suppose he had taken our tongue-tied condition to indicate complete agreement. He went stamping up some wooden stairs. 'We need keen young lads like you' he

3

bellowed over his shoulder. 'Good life this — long as you keep your nose clean — be fine — enjoy yourselves.' We both nodded eager agreement. He looked as though he could turn quite nasty without much effort.

I was seized upon first. 'Sit down there laddie' he said. Then he placed a card over my right eye. 'Just read the letters on that chart there' he commanded. I did so with ease. The same procedure followed with my left eye. He was pleased, and after satisfying himself that I had no social disease, incipient ague, or fallen arches, he said, 'That's fine laddie — fit as a fiddle.' He scribbled something on an official looking form and grinned at me. 'Well, that's about it for now.' He tapped the form with a cigarette stained finger. 'Just sign here laddie.' I signed with something of a flourish, and from that moment I was in. In with that macho lot, a gunner in the 71st Searchlight Regiment RA.

Nothing in my subsequent army service ever proceeded with such expedition as on that first brief encounter.

Unfortunately, Maurice fell at the first hurdle. The lamp post expressed dismay. 'Ah now, laddie. Bit of a snarl up here. 'Fraid I can't sign you up until next week. I see you're not eighteen 'till then. But not to worry. Come back next week and I'll see that you're put in the same detachment as your mate.'

Meanwhile, I was instructed to report for training on the following Tuesday.

Maurice also fell at the second hurdle, brought down by Sod's law. He duly presented himself, pausing only to ingratiate himself with an aggressive looking blonde at the palisade, only to be informed that an Army Council instruction received that very day, forbade further recruitment into the TA of any applicant under the age of twenty-five. This was something of a debacle. I was quite firmly in, and the door had been slammed unceremoniously in Maurice's disbelieving face.

The gleaming paragon expressed regret in a string of platitudes ending, rather lamely and ungrammatically, with the advice that, 'Orders is orders laddie.' And there ended prematurely a private quasi-military alliance. This was a pity, because there were occasions later when Maurice's dry, sardonic humour would have been a welcome antidote to the many irritants I was subsequently heir to.

Maurice got his own back later by joining the RAF.

CHAPTER 2

Cloud Cuckoo Land

Weeks flew by in a flurry of hectic and unaccustomed endeavour. On the first training session I, and assorted newcomers, were taken in hand by a sergeant to learn, of all things, how to slow march. I did wonder at the logic of the training schedule, but as the place fairly buzzed with military activity of one kind or another I assumed there was nothing more pertinent to claim the attention of mere greenhorns. So, grinning sheepishly, we marched and countermarched in untidy fashion, my mind busy with thoughts of the noble Duke of York and his ten thousand men. Indeed, our performance had about it a slight air of fantasy, but we managed to complete the exercise without falling over.

The fact that uniforms and equipment were at a premium, even at that dire period, soon became apparent. The items we did have were antiquated and almost entirely what was left over from 1918. Standard dress for training parades was fawn overalls with uniform forage caps which, but for one's

Servicing the lamp

5

Neanderthal hearing aid

right ear, would have slipped right off the head. These were the only new items. Service dress 1918 style, webbing, boots etc., appeared in the Quartermaster's store in penny packets. Men who were very tall, or quite short, had to wait months before being fully kitted out. Those extreme cases regularly besieged the QM stores in search of bits and pieces of uniform, but for week after week they were required to parade in civilian clothes and just go on hoping and wearing out their own shoes.

I had elected to join the drivers' course, reasoning vaguely, and erroneously, that being in charge of a motor vehicle gave one something of an advantage over the other squaddies. While they pounded about on the drill square a driver could lurk under the bonnet of his vehicle, look intelligent, and make a show of being busy on technical matters.

It was soon made clear to me however, that drivers were also responsible for the welfare of an enormous Lister diesel generator. This machine provided the power for the searchlight. It was a pig to start; a performance requiring the strength of two men and the patience of Job.

Apart from my own responsibilities, others were absorbing the intricacies of the lamp itself. Delicate adjustments had to be made to carbon rods to produce a good 'clean' beam. On the rare occasions when I happened to have the generator more or less under control, I was constantly harassed by demands to get the bloody volts up, or the amps down, or it may have been the other way round. I never really got to grips with my particular speciality, but somehow or other we managed to get the beam 'up'.

Then there were the 'listeners' operating antiquated sound locators. Those unfortunates grappled with a machine resembling Neanderthal man's early experiments with the development of an outsize hearing aid. These contraptions were made up of metal tubes leading from four conical shaped boxes. The open ends of the boxes picked up the throb of aircraft engines, transmitting the sound through the tubes in the manner of a rather

CLOUD CUCKOO LAND

complicated ear trumpet. Two listeners, wearing headphones, passed bearing and elevation details to the lamp operators so that the latter had a rough idea in which direction, and at what angle to point the beam.

The two 'spotters' on each detachment provided the counterweight to all this high technology. Their job was regarded as something of a sinecure; no amps or volts to fool about with, no carbon rods to curse, nothing in fact more stressful than lying prone in a kind of up-market swivelling deck chair whilst studying the night sky through binoculars. Sometimes the black void would be relieved by a sprinkling of bright stars and moonlight. In such circumstances it was an ideal pastime for budding astronomers. But when it rained, the unfortunate spotters indulged in obscenities interspersed with fervent prayers for 'stand down'.

I often wondered just what in Hell those spotters were supposed to pick out in that vast expanse of black nothing. The enemy would hardly be gracious enough to display navigation lights for our benefit.

We existed in cloud cuckoo land where everything appeared to be geared to the days of bi-planes and Zeppelins. The lads, however, made the best of what they had, although it was all relevant to making a silk purse out of a sow's ear. It was not until 1942, when radar control was implemented, that searchlights really became much more effective.

Detachment Lewis gun

7

DON'T FORGET TO WRITE

Our only offensive armament calculated to cause minor distress and anxiety to enemy flyers was a solitary Lewis gun, again a hand me down from 1918. It fired bullets effectively and made a satisfying racket, but I felt that against aircraft it left something to be desired. Nevertheless we all had a go on the firing range in the Pennines which, if nothing else, gave the sheep something to think about.

CHAPTER 3
Overture & Beginners

Spring gave way to a long warm summer as we sweated our way through exercises, lectures, square bashing and rifle drill. The laconic Sergeant Twine (Twiney when he wasn't listening) probably suffered more than his pupils. The clatter of a dropped rifle brought forth from him a deep sigh of resignation. Then, with an imploring glance heavenwards, he would groan, 'Well, for Christ's sake pick the bloody thing up then.'

Slowly, out of all the apparent chaos, order and purpose blossomed. The Regimental jig-saw took shape, notwithstanding the motley crew that we were. Bus drivers, labourers, clerks, professional men et al., all of disparate backgrounds and interests gradually came together in common effort creating, to the surprise of many, a moderately efficient unit. The plague of poor or unavailable equipment had little adverse effect on attitudes. On the contrary, we became more confident as training progressed and, tutored as we were by a number of experienced old soldiers, we felt we were making the grade. We youngsters, wet behind the ears, owed a considerable debt to the old sweats who wore the ribbons of that earlier butchery.

They quietly put us right when we floundered, and were always ready with advice, support and encouragement. Above all, they taught us to laugh when a situation appeared most unfunny. Sadly, the vast majority of those remarkable men will have been 'gathered' by now, but their contribution to our training and general welfare is remembered with affection.

On the international scene at that time, British and French politicians appeared to have lost touch with reality. Part of Czechoslovakia had been handed to Hitler as one might throw a bone to a snarling dog. The dictator subsequently demonstrated his appreciation by annexing the rest of that sad country.

Details of this unpromising period are well documented. Prime Minister Chamberlain was, in some quarters, reviled for his appeasement policy. But it is perhaps only fair to say that he was obsessed by a desire to avoid a repetition of the senseless butchery of 1914/18. That he failed reflects no discredit on the man, or his principles. And one should remember that on his return from Munich with that forlorn piece of paper, a large section of press and public alike made their great joy and support abundantly clear.

France, anxious and irresolute as ever, prevaricated and dithered. Meanwhile, the only leader in control of events, Adolf Hitler, hastened to put the finishing touches to his plans for Armageddon.

On the 14th of August 1939 I received a calling out notice from the Regiment, requiring me to present myself at the barracks at 1100 hours on the 9th of September. A footnote advised, 'Should you not present yourself on that day you will be liable to be proceeded against.' A dire enough warning, but who cared? This was it; our first annual camp. Two whole weeks away from my desk and getting paid for it into the bargain. This would surely make the groupies sit up and take notice. I had a vision of tearful farewells, and a vigorous, enthusiastic welcome on our triumphant return. But it was not to be; the wheels were about to fall off.

We pretended not to notice that preparations for war were gathering momentum. In the city, members of the services humping packs and kit bags, trudged between stations on their way to postings. Even confirmed optimists had to accept that something extremely nasty was about to burst upon us. When shortly it did so, few were ready for it.

The morning of the 24th of August 1939 was much the same as any other day. At the office there was some desultory conversation about cricket before we settled down at our high desks for another day of pen pushing, and endless arithmetic. I teetered and fidgeted on my tall stool, hopelessly urging forward the lunch break, oblivious to the fact that within hours my cosy, boring little world would shortly be in complete disarray.

Our chief accountant Arthur Barnes started it. His portly figure rolled over to my desk and he put a hand on my shoulder. 'Alfred,' he said. 'I think you ought to get off home lad. I hear that Territorials are being mustered. It can't be long before they send for you, so I think you should get off home right away.' I needed no second bidding and was out of my chair in some haste.

As I emerged from the cloakroom, mac over my arm, he was waiting for me. We shook hands. 'Good luck laddie' he said quietly, 'Off you go, and don't forget to write.' It may have sounded as though I was just off on holiday, and indeed, as far as I was concerned, and in my foolish ignorance, I believed that to be so.

When I arrived home mother immediately assumed I had been sacked. She had an endearing facility for jumping to dismal conclusions. The son and heir had returned home unexpectedly, hours before he was due, *ergo*, he had been sacked. It was all in tune with mother's maxim that every silver lining had a cloud.

OVERTRURE & BEGINNERS

> **Army Form E 623.**
> Not to be maintained in duplicate.
>
> ## TERRITORIAL ARMY.
> (COAST DEFENCE AND ANTI-AIRCRAFT UNITS.)
>
> ### IMMEDIATE AND IMPORTANT.—NOTICE TO JOIN.
>
> No., Rank and Name _1451217 Howarth A._
>
> Unit _71 S/L Regt_ ROYAL REGIMENT OF ARTILLERY.
>
> Whereas in the present national emergency the Secretary of State has authorised the calling out of officers and men of {Coast Defence* / Anti-Aircraft} units of the Territorial Army in accordance with agreements entered into by them under Section 13 (2) (b) of the Territorial and Reserve Forces Act, 1907, you are hereby required to report immediately at _the Drill Hall, Thursday 8PM_
>
> Should you not present yourself as ordered, you will be liable to be proceeded against.
>
> Place _FAILSWORTH_ _Bloggs_
> _Adjutant._
> _p/Adjutant 71st Searchlight Regt. R.A._
>
> Time _____
>
> Date _2 4 AUG 1939_ Unit.
>
> *Strike out the words not applicable.
>
> N.B.—This notice to be sent by hand or by registered post in a plain envelope. (A.F. D419 will not be used.)

The summons (calling out notice)

Hardly had I settled down to explain before an army despatch rider drew up at the gate and popped a brown envelope through the letter box. It was another blue form inviting me, in forceful terms, to present myself at the barracks 'forthwith'. The usual dire threats were included in the footnote.

11

It seemed that our chief accountant's prescience had at least given me a head start.

Fortunately father was on early turn from his railway duties, and together we spent a frustrating hour or so trying to sort out my equipment. I had no idea how all the webbing straps fitted together. It was largely a case of trial and error. The trials were conducted in my bedroom out of deference to mother, who was on the settee having a fit of the vapours muttering, 'I told you so didn't I?' every few minutes. Silver linings were quite out of it now.

Father and I became rather irritable as we struggled to get it all together. It was not so much due to the equipment, but I was experiencing the first indications of nascent alarm, and father, who had seen it all before, was probably regretting his cheerful lies about the possibility of war.

Some time later, hung about with packs and all manner of warlike appurtenances, I clumped downstairs. Already the new boots nagged at my heels, and they creaked if I so much as took a deep breath. I caught a glimpse of myself in a mirror. It was not a pretty sight. The reflection brought to mind the old Duke of Wellington's observation on his own troops, 'I don't know what they do to the enemy, but by God they frighten me!' I knew what he meant.

Downstairs there was some brittle chit-chat, but time was passing. 'Forthwith', the notice had said, and it was about time to say the awkward goodbyes.

The solemnity of the moment was relieved briefly when I became jammed in the doorway with my lumpy equipment. But the atmosphere was strained. What was there to say? Father could think only of writing, 'Now don't forget to write — soon as you get settled' a sentence he repeated half a dozen times on my way to the gate. Mother was more pragmatic. 'Now mind what you're doing. Remember to change your socks, and for goodness' sake mind you don't get wet.' We were never an outwardly demonstrative family so, thankfully, there was no kissing. I just grinned, waved, and went creaking up the street.

At half past midnight, to all round surprise and excitement, I was back, noisily clamouring at the front door. Mother hastened down probably hoping I had been peremptorily dismissed as being unfit for any form of warlike activity. Father was wandering about in his pyjamas, sleepily demanding to know what the hell they were all playing at. But war had not yet been declared, and the truth was that having summoned the troops, no-one quite knew what they ought to do with us. We were a temporary

OVERTRURE & BEGINNERS

embarrassment. And so, for the immediate future, it was a cosy arrangement of home comforts; at least I was able to sleep in my own bed for a while.

The scene at the barracks that night had been chaotic. Several hundred bewildered soldiery milled about for hours awaiting further orders; a condition which became quite commonplace over the years. Grim faced officers and NCO's bearing clip boards rushed hither and yon. Names were called and men despatched to far corners of the parade ground, only to be called back within minutes, or completely forgotten about.

Fortunately, as peace of a sort still prevailed, the area was illuminated. The night was warm and still. Those men not receiving conflicting orders sat about in anxious, uncertain groups. Some talked in low tones and handed round cigarettes. Others joked nervously. Some stretched out on the hard ground and slept, surrounded by their kit.

Shortly before midnight I was detailed to mount guard at the palisade; a duty I would have jumped at earlier, but by that time all the groupies had sensibly cleared off to their beds. The only defensive weapon I possessed at that moment was my swagger cane. I suppose that, *in extremis*, I could have used it to beat the brains out of any intruder not wearing a helmet.

Half an hour later a sergeant appeared to inform me that it was no bloody good standing there. I was instructed to report to a harassed officer who immediately told me to return home and re-present myself at 0900 hours the following morning, adding some unnecessary details about what would happen should I elect not to report. He needn't have worried. The military machine already had me firmly in its maw.

The days passed in agreeable fashion as far as I was concerned. Reporting for duty each morning, and bedding down at home in the evening, I rejoiced in the knowledge that back at the office they would be up to their ears in the dreaded month end balance; a procedure fraught with anxiety and recrimination when the inevitable discrepancy was discovered.

I felt that these were halcyon days, but it did not require an Einstein to figure that time was fast running out.

At the end of the week, on September 1st, Germany cut loose, launching its massive forces against Poland. It was immediately obvious from the intense activity at the barracks that the balloon was about to take to the air.

On Sunday morning, 3rd of September, the Regiment assembled for the first church parade. It was a drumhead service on the parade ground. Base drums from the Regimental Band were draped in the Union flag, forming the traditional altar and altar cloth. Captain Hughes, the Padre, on that occasion took the service.

DON'T FORGET TO WRITE

A light breeze ruffled the Padre's cassock and lifted a corner of the flag as he began to speak. Captain Hughes was not a young man, and this morning his friendly face was sombre and drawn. Then, fidgeting with his notes, he made the announcement we had all been expecting; that war had been declared.

So we were at it once again. A mere 21 years after all the killing and maiming of 1914/18 we were about to cross the Rubicon once more.

The interim period had not been one of prosperity. For those who had returned from the slaughter, those for whom a politician had coined the promising phrase 'homes fit for heroes', there was rife unemployment, and the homes never materialised. Many of those heroes had taken to the streets, grey faced men not long out of the trenches, some on crutches, parading in the gutter singing for pennies. And now, just as things were beginning to pick up, Hitler had put the clock back; back to the misery our fathers knew only too well.

I glanced to right and left at faces that a few months previously had been unfamiliar, and now we were united in friendship, or comradeship, or a bit of both. I wanted to see what reaction there might be. But there was none. The lads continued to stare at the altar, busy with their thoughts. My own thoughts centered on my parents. Mother would probably be repeating, 'I told you so, didn't I?' as if it were all father's fault!

Padre Hughes, after some predictable talk about doing one's duty and so on, brought the drumhead service to a close with Henry Francis Lyte's hymn, *Abide with Me*.

As we marched off I could see that one of our gunners, a very tall individual, was on parade in his best civvy suit. Obviously the quartermaster still had no uniform to fit the man. Yet here we were, off to fight a war against an enemy armed and kitted out with first class equipment, and we were unable to find a uniform for a tall gunner, not even a left over from 1918.

I just hoped that He had been listening to our hymn. Britain was shortly going to need all the help it could muster.

CHAPTER 4

Curtain Up

The lights went out and stayed out for the duration. People barged painfully into lamp posts, cursing each other's blindness, and that bastard Hitler as they groped their way about. Some of those feeling their way touched bodies in places that, in other circumstances, would have had them in a police cell.

But as the months passed, with no immediate sign of the aerial onslaught we had been expecting, the use of shaded torches made life a little easier for pedestrians. Some motorists however scared the hell out of pedestrians and themselves by unexpectedly mounting an unseen kerb.

I was to find out for myself all about the hazards of night driving sooner than expected. My cushy period of lodging at home came to an end late one dark, moonless night, when I was posted to a detachment.

My immediate task was to drive a ten ton generator lorry loaded with men and equipment to a place of whose precise, or even approximate location, I stood in complete ignorance. The Detachment Commander looked worried, as well he might. Not only did he not know quite where his destination lay, he was also blissfully unaware that I had previously only driven a lorry a couple of times round the town. I felt it unwise to burden him further at that moment, so I kept my mouth shut!

The situation clarified when the Battery Sergeant Major materialised out of the gloom demanding to know if we had taken bloody root. He stabbed a finger at a point on the map, which turned out to be Standish Hall just outside Wigan, and sent us on our tentative way.

In terms of distance from barracks, the journey to Wigan was negligible. It was the bit in between that has lodged in my memory over the years.

We jerked our way out on to the main road to the accompaniment of loud and expensive sounding noises from the gearbox with which I was trying to come to terms. (Those of you who have known only synchromesh don't know what you missed!) Progress was marked by a loud mechanical screech every time I touched the gear lever. Those civilians tucked up in bed may well have imagined a column of tanks moving out under cover of darkness, such was the racket.

DON'T FORGET TO WRITE

The Detachment Commander, by virtue of his rank, occupied the front passenger seat. Dark it certainly was, but I could see that his right hand gripped the seat, whilst his left hand rested on the door handle; a clear indication that my driving suggested the possible necessity of a sharpish exit. The men in the back were unusually quiet too. Normally they would entertain with questionable songs and ditties, but I think our erratic progress that night put the fear of God into them. It didn't do me much good either. But what could they expect from an 18 year old tyro whose experience with heavy lorries was at best ephemeral.

Miraculously, notwithstanding my dubious driving, map reading disabilities, and the overwhelming blackness surrounding us, we managed to locate the tree lined drive leading down to the Hall. In the ghostly silence of that first night I bedded down in the lorry. I was beginning to learn the truth about 'Roughing it'. I huddled in my greatcoat for what seemed a very long night of cramps and nightmares, and I was not sorry to see the grey light of dawn filtering through the trees.

The morning wasn't much better. It started with a wash and shave in a bucket of cold water, followed by a breakfast consisting of what appeared to be an unholy union of haggis and coagulated porridge. The cook slopped the stuff into our mess tins, pausing every now and then to scratch vigorously at his crotch; presumably he had located a foreign body there.

The day was enlivened somewhat by visitations from a bewildering variety of officers and NCOs all checking upon our readiness for action. They all went away, if not satisfied, at least full of hope.

Detachment life was decidedly uncomfortable and restrictive. The generator lorry lurked under a canopy of trees some distance from the rest of the detachment. This was my world. The lorry was my bedroom and dining room. I could leave it only at meal times, but then, balancing the cook's latest gastronomic obscenity in two mess tins I was required to retire to my home from home without delay.

During those early days we were ordered to remain fully dressed at all times. Presumably higher command did not intend us to be caught with our pants down.

We were not allowed off the site for any reason under pain of severe punishment. There was an inviting pub just down the road, and I knew that many of the lads who were gasping for a pint would have happily sold their grandmothers into slavery for the chance of half an hour at the bar.

Some detachment commanders on the more remote sites did take a chance and allowed one or two desperate individuals to slip the leash for a quick one. It had to be quick because we never knew when the orderly officer might pay a sly visit.

Change was in the air constantly. More sites were set up and detachments moved around. Men came and went, and the dreary routine persisted. Air sentry duty (two hours on, four off), occasional practice 'exposures', maintenance work and trying to keep clothing and one's self clean with only a bucket of cold water all kept the lads in that odd, semi-mutinous condition peculiar to squaddies everywhere.

Some weeks passed. We had more or less settled down to detachment life at the Hall when we were abruptly given our marching orders; pack up and report to RHQ forthwith. (All army orders ended with 'forthwith'.) This was one of those unheralded moves which proved to be fundamental to army life; wait until a unit has thoroughly settled down — then move it somewhere else.

Our journey back to RHQ was blessed with daylight, and by that time I had to some extent made peace with the gears. The mechanical screech that had so enlivened the journey down occurred but rarely.

We swept into barracks with some panache, to be greeted by a sergeant major who looked puzzled. 'Who,' he demanded, 'are you lot then?' After some discussion and waving of arms, the sergeant major said, 'Right, you lucky people, parade for FFI and inoculation fourteen hundred sharp.' The FFI (free from infection) seemed fair enough. Apparently we were about to have our first real medical examination. Inoculations, however, were regarded with grave suspicion. There appeared to be general apprehension about having needles stuck into our arms, or anywhere else for that matter, and the prospect caused some muttering amongst the troops.

The FFI came first. We all stood in line completely naked, while a bespectacled medical officer moved along the line nonchalantly seizing each man's private parts, at the same time commanding the soldier to cough. Some of the younger lads at first thought they were in the hands (literally) of some pervert of a medical officer — until the strange procedure was explained by an older squaddie.

This line-up of naked, goose pimpled soldiery was hardly an impressive sight. It was for many, the first experience of massed nakedness and some embarrassment was evident. One or two of the younger ones coughed in genteel fashion more appropriate to the Athenaeum, thereby irritating the MO who then took a firmer grip saying, '*Cough* man *cough!* Don't just clear your throat.'

... **fire burn and cauldron bubble**

The inoculation parade formed a crocodile of fifty or so nervous individuals outside the MO's hut.

In attendance were two cynical looking medical orderlies wearing white jackets. We were all nervous and fidgety, intimidated by stories of blunt needles and assurances that we would all soon be sick as dogs for a week or more.

Regimental Sergeant Major Ruddick, well aware of our misgivings, seized the opportunity to harangue the assembly. Striding up and down the line, slapping his thigh with a swagger cane, he paused to denounce us all. 'Namby pambies, the lot of you. Never seen such a miserable collection. Scared of a bit of a prick.' (At this, one or two lads thought he was referring to the MO.) He continued in his forthright denunciation until an orderly came out to inform him that the MO was ready for him. Ruddick turned on his heel, and with a parting, evil grin, disappeared into the hut.

After a brief interval we heard a faint thump from within. A moment later the two orderlies re-appeared bearing a stretcher upon which lay our intrepid RSM. He was out cold, and there were those who feared he might be dead, and others who feared he might not be. He recovered quickly of course, but for one reason or another we saw little of him for a week or two.

My detachment was shortly posted to a site at Grasscroft in the hills north of Oldham. Here we were well looked after by the local people who regularly brought jugs of tea and generally made us welcome.

There was just one lady though, whose attitude was less than helpful. She lived close to the site, and Eddie Harrison who had commanded a detachment there, told me that whenever his lads passed her house she would run out, shake her fist, and shout 'Murderers!' The reason for the outburst was due to the fact that reflection from the searchlight beam fell upon her house, prompting the hysterical claim that German pilots would spot her 'des res' and proceed to bomb it! The lads took her ravings in their stride and ignored the woman.

At Grasscroft, I once again reigned in splendid isolation with my generator lorry situated in the corner of a field at the bottom of a rough lane. I had to traipse up and down the lane some four hundred yards or so each way to pick up my meal from the cookhouse. By the time I staggered back to the lorry with two mess tins, I had usually lost most of the tea, and what remained had gone cold, along with the main course. Then I had to trudge back for pudding which, if we were lucky, would be 'Spotted Dick', an unwholesome but filling mess of suet dotted with currants.

I was told of a cook who, being short of a suitable cloth, used an empty sandbag in which to cook a 'Spotted Dick'. When it was served up, the lads cheerfully picked out the strands of hessian as they ate. To turn down 'Spotted Dick' would have been unthinkable!

Some cooks were good, but ours, arbitrarily chosen from 12 men, would have been thrown out of a scout camp.

Stories about army cooks are legion, but the one related by the late Eric Barber MBE, takes first prize. Eric was our Troop Sergeant Major, and on one of his tours of inspection came across a detachment cook preparing to boil potatoes in petrol, and that over an open fire! No one knows how close the lads came to having roast potatoes, with possibly a barbecued cook on the side. The cook excused himself by claiming he had no sense of smell! Eric told him he had no bloody sense full stop.

We were never short of visitors to the Grasscroft site. Every evening local girls came round to chat, and it was then that my isolated location came to be envied by the rest of the detachment. But girls were not our only visitors. The Troop Officer and his sergeant were occasional nocturnal prowlers who tended to materialise out of the darkness, usually in the small hours. The air sentry's job related more to keeping a sharp look-out for these disturbing visitors than watching for the master site's beam, but we were nevertheless caught out one dark night.

On that occasion it was my good fortune to be off duty, curled up in blanket and greatcoat on the floor of the lorry, trying to keep warm. I heard nothing and unfortunately neither did the sentry.

The first indication that anything was amiss came when the door of the hut burst open, and the bombardier found himself staring bleary eyed down the barrel of the detachment Lewis gun. The Troop Officer had cunningly slipped through a hedge from the main road, lifted the gun from its mounting, then stalked the sentry, poised to seize an opportunity to pounce. When it came he sprang into the hut like the pantomime demon king, causing alarm and consternation all round. Several heads had to roll as a consequence.

I had troubles of my own at this time though. The new unyielding army boots wrought havoc on my tender heels and I now possessed a cluster of extremely painful and bloody blisters. Any movement at all was agonising, and I stumbled about like an android with a blown fuse. The idea of reporting sick did not appeal to my vanity, so I continued to grimace and groan my way up and down the lane.

Fortunately for me, circumstances had changed to the extent that one or two men were to be allowed some hours leave of absence. When my turn came, father rolled up in the old Morris to take me home.

When he saw me doing my zombie act, which I probably overdid for his benefit, he bundled me into the car and shot off homeward.

Father had always been rather good at first aid, and no sooner were we home than he whipped off my boots and socks. My heels resembled two pieces of raw liver. Even father was aghast. Mother clutched her forehead and went for a lie down.

The expert ministrations worked like a charm and within days the spring had more or less returned to my step.

CHAPTER 5

Breathing Space

The 'Phoney War' went on, and with the onset of winter I was posted to the troop headquarters site perched atop Tandle Hill. This exposed and draughty site was situated a couple of miles south of Rochdale. It was an ideal site for the purpose, affording a clear all round siting through 360 degrees. Over to the east the Pennines loomed darkly, and to the south the stark Manchester skyline could be seen clearly.

On Tandle Hill we were fortunate to have an amiable Troop Officer, a good cook, and hutted accommodation, a desirable trinity not often realised.

My job there was to man the telephone link with Battery and Regimental HQ. Limited manpower meant there was no one to relieve me, which meant sitting up all night keeping the field telephone company, listening to grunts and an occasional fart issuing from the other side of a flimsy partition where slept the Troop Officer.

His sleeping accommodation was quite basic and I could hear every creak as his portly figure tossed and turned, putting severe strain on his camp bed.

That I should fall asleep quite often was perhaps understandable in the circumstances. I had only to wedge myself in the corner by the stove, stretch out my legs, and very soon I was away, oblivious to the snoring and farting. Now and again I was dimly aware of the officer's pyjamas clad bulk striding carefully over my outstretched legs as he made his way out for a pee. Why he never reprimanded me for sleeping on duty I never understood; on the contrary he was always most careful not to disturb my slumbers.

This was the winter of the big snowfall, as if the Country were not in enough trouble. It was my good fortune to have scrounged a half day's leave, and it was during my absence that snow almost completely obliterated the site. I returned in late evening, having cadged a lift in a doctor's car. We only just made it. I was alarmed to find the lane leading up to the site completely blocked. There was no alternative other than teeter along the top of a stone wall to make some progress. I fell off frequently and half lay in chest high snow cursing my luck. The dense white blanket had me in its chilly embrace so often that I found myself shrugging off mild panic. There was not a soul in sight, nor a sound from anywhere. It was an eerie sensation and I was relieved eventually to stagger wearily into the men's hut. One man lying on his bed reading a comic said, 'Bloody 'ell look — Father Christmas already and I 'aven't 'ung up me stocking yet!'

Some weeks after the snow cleared, the Troop Officer sent for me. I was to be given a formal driving test that afternoon, and subject to my passing, I would be posted to RHQ, as the Adjutant's driver. I couldn't imagine why the Adjutant, of all people, would want to trust a mere 18 year old to ferry him about, but I wasn't arguing, it sounded as though it could be a cushy number.

I passed the test without any problems and returned to the 'Hill' to pack. The ration truck took me back to RHQ, where I nervously reported for duty in my new job.

Captain T. A. Milns was my boss, and whatever misgivings I might have entertained were quickly dispelled. I found him to be gentlemanly and amiable, and as the weeks passed I began thoroughly to enjoy my new job. It was in many ways an interesting experience from which I learned a great deal in more ways than one. I was privy to conversations of both a military and sometimes highly personal nature, often illuminating, but I had the sense to keep my mouth shut at all times.

Each morning, standing by for instructions, I spent some time fiddling about with the car, trying to look important and busy. In this I was not entirely successful however. Apparently RSM Ruddick had his beady eye on me.

In that characteristic springy step he bore down upon me, and I could see from a distance that he was at battle stations. 'Why,' he demanded, 'were you not on parade this morning? I ought to put you on a charge for being absent, and if you're not on first parade tomorrow I shall do just that. So you be on parade tomorrow — or else. Understand me?' He waved his swagger cane under my nose and sprang off in search of other prey.

I understood perfectly, and saddled now with this interesting predicament I should have to lay aside my finer feelings and unburden myself to the Adjutant at the earliest.

Later that morning I tittle-tattled away as we drove off. The boss smiled a grim smile and said comfortingly, 'Don't worry about it. You're my driver, and I give the orders. You are not to attend any parades until I say otherwise.'

I suspected that shortly after our return to barracks the RSM was put through the mangle. He never bothered me again, but whenever we met,

BREATHING SPACE

his complexion took on a russet hue, and I knew he was thinking, 'Sodding little tell-tale.' Never mind, I was off the hook, but felt it prudent henceforth to exhibit all the soldierly qualities I could muster.

The 'Phoney War' period gave us a breathing space to polish up our act, but it did induce an unfortunate sense of complacency in many.

When that rather daft song, 'We're going to hang out the washing on the Siegfried line' first made its appearance, I had an uncomfortable feeling that we could well have reason to regret the sentiments expressed long before we started hammering at Germany's door. As things turned out I wasn't far wrong.

The Norwegian debacle was a sure indicator of what we were up against. The Germans certainly lost many warships, but after some six weeks of fighting, again with our completely inadequate equipment relative to the conditions, we were firmly kicked out. Even Winston Churchill described it as a ramshackle campaign.

CHAPTER 6

Red Alert

On the 10th of May 1940 German forces blasted their way into Holland and Belgium with thunderclap surprise, overwhelming both countries with fearsome fire power and the skilful use of determined parachutists. Simultaneously an armoured thrust with close air support burst through the weakly held front at Sedan. Within hours German tanks were roaming the area behind the French lines creating havoc. From that bloody nose at Sedan the French never recovered, and by the end of May it was all over bar the shouting.

Operation DYNAMO, the evacuation of troops cornered in the Dunkirk area, commenced on the 16th of May. 861 ships of all kinds were engaged in the project, of which 249 were sunk. This astounding operation resulted in 338,000 troops being returned to this country.

After the Dunkirk dust had settled attitudes changed. There was now nothing of substance between Britain and the enemy save the English Channel, yet perversely, people spoke together in terms of sheer bravado. I doubt whether the possibility of imminent defeat occurred to anyone. On the contrary, our parlous situation drew the population together as never before, and a new mateyness and determination took over.

Few had any illusions about the realities of our position. We were about to pay the piper in, to quote Winston Churchill's timeless phrase, 'Blood, Toil, Tears and Sweat'. Winston may not have been a military genius, but his tremendous energy, courage and determination, allied to brilliant oratory, roused the people to new heights of courage and endeavour.

Air raids, directed at the civil population and RAF airfields became commonplace. Many fighter airfields were badly damaged and for a time it was touch and go with our fighter defence.

As if all this were not bad enough, we had the prospect of a German invasion to concentrate our minds. Barges were reported to be assembling in large numbers along the French coast, and corresponding German troop movements indicated the real possibility of an early assault upon the South coast.

RED ALERT

Meanwhile, on the 10th of June, the fat opportunist Mussolini declared war on Britain and France. Fearful that all the bargains would go before he got in on the act, he begged Hitler to allow Italian bombers to join in the assault on the 'Inglesi'. He got his wish, and lost most of his bombers in the process.

Air raids, increasing over the months in tempo and severity, became more and more of an unpleasant feature of our lives. The searchlights were busy, but the antiquated equipment was hardly fitted for the task, at least in those early days, and we had little success in picking off enemy planes.

Meanwhile, the prospect of a sea and airborne assault was an ever present concern.

I drove into barracks one warm sultry evening to find everyone at panic stations. An invasion 'Red' alert had been received. All troops were being armed and posted for defence with all speed. At the time it all seemed unreal, more especially as I was issued with a ·22 rifle and a handful of ammunition. I was directed to the adjacent churchyard, there to take up a defensive position.

I crouched behind the most substantial headstone I could find, although the possibility of parachutists attacking a graveyard seemed to me to be fairly remote. As the minutes ticked by I had time to ponder upon the likely effect my peashooter of a rifle would have against some buck paratrooper and his Schmeisser. I conjured up visions of my ·22 rounds pinging harmlessly off his steel helmet.

Mind you, my ·22 was an advance on some of the defensive equipment being issued that night. Eric Barber, MBE, in his book, *My War*, tells of the issue to his troop of some 70 pikes! It was left to Sergeant Major Barber to work out how he proposed to employ them. In the absence of official guidance Eric gave instructions to bury the shafts in the ground at an angle in the form of a makeshift palisade. (Shades of Agincourt!)

Fortunately my martial capabilities were not put to the test, and after a couple of hours or so, to general relief, we were stood down.

The bombing increased in tempo, and shortly the Regiment was transferred to the Liverpool area which was then suffering a regular pasting.

RHQ occupied Mather Avenue barracks, a stone's throw from Penny Lane, but long years before the latter's association with the Beatles.

462 Battery moved to Thurstaston on the Wirral peninsula, occupying a colony of wooden holiday chalets. The location was much envied by some of the troops who were stuck out on such sites as Gladstone Dock.

RHQ Mather Avenue, Liverpool

RED ALERT

This latter was perhaps the most vulnerable of sites. Here one of our men was killed during a particularly severe raid.

The new station at Mather Avenue barracks, a fairly modern building, proved to be quite an improvement on the old mill in Thorley Street. We had decent iron beds, a dining room, a spacious indoor drill area, and a badminton court. But above all else we had acquired a cook *par excellence*. His name escapes me now, but the food he turned out remains in my fond memory. He cooked like an angel. What is more he often doled out second helpings, thereby endearing himself to all his comrades.

A new padre joined us in Liverpool. We found him to be surprisingly aloof, even on the weekly church parades, and very soon our jaundiced view of the new man of God hardened considerably when he put his driver on a charge, threatening him with the full rigours of military discipline.

The charge resulted from an incident that occurred when his driver was demonstrating basic driving techniques to one of the men in the Padre's open topped Austin 8. The official driver sat in the passenger seat, instructing his pupil in the use of clutch and accelerator. All this was taking place in one of the spacious garages directly opposite loading bays whose platforms stood some four feet or so from ground level. The inevitable happened. Pupil stuck his foot on the accelerator and the car shot forward, burying itself with an almighty crash beneath the loading bay opposite.

The upper works of the car were completely sliced off, and we expected to find a couple of headless corpses. Fortunately they had both ducked in the nick of time and were safe enough, but completely trapped. We let down the tyres and managed to drag out the battered car and its shaken occupants.

At the subsequent inquiry, chaired by the Adjutant, we laid a smoke screen of white lies, insisting that the official driver had been at the wheel, and that his foot must have slipped. I doubt if we were altogether believed, and clearly the Adjutant had his suspicions. He called me back twice to further quiz me, but I stuck to my guns and we heard no more.

The Padre's violent reaction rather soured his already tentative relationship with the troops; we felt that a little Christian charity would not have been out of place in the circumstances.

Shortly after this contretemps we heard that the NCO in charge of petrol and oil issues had been removed following a spot check on supplies. Whether he was perhaps inefficient, or dishonest, or even both, was never made clear, but when the Adjutant sent for me and put me in immediate charge of petrol issues, he made it quite clear that I would henceforth be responsible for balancing the books. 'I don't care how you do it Howarth,' he said, grinning at me, 'but I expect you to sort it all out and report back. I'll leave it to you.'

We both knew there was only one way to make up the shortfall in petrol — drivers were soon going to notice a sharp fall in miles per gallon.

At Mather Avenue petrol was dispensed from an archaic hand pump operated by a handle. The drivers had an idea of what was going on and watched me carefully, counting the number of turns of the handle. Sometimes I distracted their attention by saying that a tyre on the other side was soft, or that Sergeant Houlker was looking for them. But this subterfuge succeeded for only a day or so, and soon drivers were vociferous in their complaints. 'Hey, give that bloody handle another turn. That's nothing like a gallon you bugger!' I remained unmoved, secure in the knowledge that my brief left no room for generosity.

I was going about my business in the oil store one morning with, as was my habit, an empty pipe clenched between my teeth, when Major Marshall the second in command bustled in. His face was thunderous as he pointed to a large notice forbidding smoking or naked lights. 'I'm putting you on a charge', he announced. 'It states quite clearly no smoking and you are contravening standing orders.' I took the pipe out to show him it was quite empty of tobacco, but he was not to be put off his stroke. 'You're on a charge', he bellowed, and stumped off to his office.

Some drivers within earshot of this exchange were vastly amused. They felt I was getting my come-uppance for short changing them on petrol issues. I was not amused.

Major Marshall was autocratic and enigmatic; somewhat aloof from the *hoi polloi*. The men, therefore, appeared always to be wary of him. This was unfortunate, but he had endured the carnage of 1914/18 and perhaps that fact excuses any perceived shortcomings.

The following morning I was summoned to the Major's office. On the way I speculated upon what further charges he might have conjured up. In the event he delivered a mild lecture all about setting an example to the others, and informed me that he was not proceeding with the charge.

In due course I was able to report to the Adjutant that the books at last balanced; there were no discrepancies of any kind. He looked suitably relieved and treated me to a verbal pat on the back for my efforts. The drivers were also relieved; the vehicles were about to return acceptable fuel consumption figures.

RED ALERT

The dominant feature of life in Liverpool at that time was, of course, the regularity and ferocity of bombing raids. Quite often it was necessary to drive through the city at the height of a raid. The feeble lights of the car were quite useless. It was often a matter of feeling the way forward at a crawl, bumping over fire hoses and trying to avoid scattered debris.

On all sides buildings sprouted gouts of flame. Smoke and blazing embers drifted across the roadway, and silhouetted against the leaping red and yellow flames, steel helmeted firemen and wardens performed a kind of *danse macabre*. Over the din of explosions and crashing masonry the tingling bells of ambulances added a sombre note to the Danté-esque scene.

One memorable night, on my lonely way back from Gladstone Dock, I happened to be in the shadow of the Liver Building, and apparently surrounded by flames and smoke and general mayhem. As I sought a passage through the fires and debris, I had an opportunity to witness the end of one of our tormentors. The plane was ablaze, scattering sparks as it spiralled slowly down to splash into the Mersey. The spectacle left me completely unmoved, except perhaps for a feeling of satisfaction that at least the gunners now had something to crow about.

I was fortunate enough to be given leave over the Christmas period 1940, and the prospect of turning my back on all the noise and wreckage appealed to me no end as I was beginning to get a bit fed up with it all. I suppose I could be described, in the jargon of the day, as a touch 'Bomb Happy'.

It was good to be home at last, and I was enjoying the peace and quiet of Sunday the 22nd of December when, just after 6.30 pm the sirens started their banshee howl on the night air. I could scarcely believe it, but perhaps it would turn out to be a false alarm after all. Far from being a false alarm however, the wailing sirens signalled the start of a massive and vicious blitz on Manchester.

The attack continued over two nights, bringing in its train the deaths of many civilians, destruction of many familiar and well loved landmarks, and untold misery to thousands. So much for the short, peaceful break I had so looked forward to!

Manchester and Salford took a severe beating over those two nights. It seemed to us, some four miles north, that the city was ablaze from end to end. When dawn broke after the last bomber had left, some thirty-odd acres of the city centre had been devastated. Many hundreds of civilians, police, nurses, wardens and firemen, all engaged on their respective duties, died violently during the onslaught.

Getting back to Liverpool immediately following the raids presented a problem. Central station was out of action, as was Exchange, and part of Victoria.

As I walked away desperately seeking some form of transport, I was struck by the appearance of exhausted firemen. Grey faced, covered in dust, they leaned on their equipment, trying to get some rest. But their eyes were wide open, seeing nothing — save perhaps a re-run of the horrors of the previous 48 hours.

After wandering about aimlessly for some time, I managed to cadge a lift in a lorry. There were many detours due to blocked roads, and eventually I was obliged to cover the last few miles on foot.

CHAPTER 7

New Pastures

As winter progressed, the grape vine picked up persistent rumours that the Regiment was scheduled for re-location. This prompted a good deal of misinformed speculation of course. We were going south proclaimed one of our barrack room know-alls. Others were said to have glimpsed orders despatching us to the East Coast defences.

None succeeded in divining the true destination which, when it became officially known, raised a few eyebrows and led to an excited perusal of school atlases.

Of all locations speculated upon, the Orkney Islands were undreamt of. We all knew of course that Scapa Flow was the base for the Home Fleet at that time, and there was general satisfaction in the knowledge that the 71st was to play a small part in defending the anchorage.

Although the majority of the lads knew little about the topography of the Islands, we all remembered that the battleship *Royal Oak* had been sunk there one dark October night in 1939, with the tragic loss of 800 lives.

The Old Man of Hoy — a familiar sight to all those approaching Orkney

DON'T FORGET TO WRITE

We had no illusions about our future part in the defence of the Islands, but whatever form it took, it would surely be better than watching a city being taken apart and being able to do very little about it.

462 Battery went by rail to Thurso, the railhead on the northern tip of Scotland, thence by ferry, the venerable *Earl of Zetland*, to Stromness. 463 Battery and RHQ were taken by rail to Aberdeen, where we boarded ship bound for Kirkwall, the main town on the group of Islands. RHQ occupied a windswept site overlooking Loch Kirbister. The accommodation comprised a rather battered looking house which served as officer's mess and sleeping quarters, and three or four wooden huts for administrative personnel and living quarters for the men. Significantly, each hut was secured by two steel hawsers slung over the roof. The ends of the hawsers were embedded in concrete. We had heard of the gales up there, but wondered if it were not a case of 'belt and braces'. Any such notions were quickly dispelled when a Force 10 struck shortly after our arrival.

Flayed by the shrieking wind, Loch Kirbister took on the appearance of an angry sea. In such conditions, one had to be extremely careful opening a hut door, otherwise the wind was likely to whip the door off its hinges pretty smartly.

Contrary to the feelings of most of the lads, I very soon fell in love with the Islands. The very wildness of our surroundings appealed to me, and even the weather, which could be quite foul, seldom bothered me. Indeed I rather enjoyed the often dramatic swings between raging storms and fitful sunlight.

During the winter months daylight was with us but briefly, and the dark storm lashed days often resulted in the lads becoming affected by severe depression. This condition was generally known as 'Orkneyitis', and manifested itself in various ways. Some of the men became morose and irritable. Others went about muttering to themselves and became quite misanthropic.

As winter gripped the Islands, those suffering from Orkneyitis were not at all charmed to be told that the Regiment was to participate in an exercise designed to test the Island's defences against an enemy landing.

I'm not sure to this day exactly what was to have been our contribution to the enterprise. Whatever it was, our officers obviously took the matter seriously, earnestly consulting maps and compasses.

Also involved in the exercise were elements of the Gordon Highlanders, Commandos, and a Canadian tank regiment. The latter were to attempt a landing under cover of darkness.

NEW PASTURES

It had to rain of course, and when it rains in Orkney, it does so horizontally. No matter what you may be wearing, it will get you in no time at all, right through to the skin.

We, that is RHQ, moved to a position some miles to the north, occupying a tatty wooden hut which leaked all over the place. Major Marshall appeared to be directing operations from a map table, surrounded by anxious junior officers. I tried to catnap on the floor of the vestibule, but every few minutes the door flew open to admit dispatch-riders and a shower of rain blasted in by the usual Force 10.

My fitful and rather damp catnapping was interrupted by someone instructing me to go off into the night and find the Gordon's HQ. My sketchy instructions indicated they were located in a cottage a few miles up the road.

The night was as black as Agamemnon's tomb, but a good deal wetter. Somehow I scraped along, keeping literally in close touch with the hedgerow until I found myself at a crossroads. There I could just make out the dim white shape of a small cottage. I stumbled and squelched down a crumbling path and hammered on the door. I should have known there was something wrong. The place appeared deserted; no voices, no sentry, nothing.

I hammered on the door again, to no effect, so I tried the latch. The door wasn't locked. In the darkened room I could make out a smouldering peat fire, but not a sign of a Gordon anywhere. It occurred to me that they had either moved on, or been taken prisoner.

The glowing fire was tempting, and I was considering the benefits of a few minutes to warm up when a slight creak behind startled me. My torch picked out an elderly couple sitting up in bed! The man wore a woollen bob hat and resembled an elderly Pinocchio. His wife wore what looked like a chambermaid's bonnet. Both were obviously terrified and speechless.

I was crestfallen. Not only had I barged unbidden into their home, I had also scared the living daylights out of them like some rampaging Hun. I tried to reassure the couple, but as I stood over the marital bed offering apologies and explanations, I could see that water from my steel helmet and greatcoat was dripping on to the old man.

I left in something of a hurry, still shouting apologies.

The Gordons were never found that night, and my negative report upon return to HQ was received with surprising indifference. The reason, I suppose, was the fact that events had overtaken us, and we were on the move again.

33

Gradually the exercise ground to a confused close. The wind had abated slightly, but the incessant rain still poured down, and we were all delighted to see Loch Kirbister again. I suppose the Gordon Highlanders were eventually discovered, but frankly we couldn't have cared less. All we wanted to do was dry out.

Sergeant Houlker came in with some good news as we huddled round the stove. 'I'll cheer you lot up' he said, smirking at us. 'You're all going to get a rum ration shortly, and I shall be dishing it out, so don't think it's going to be a free booze-up.' We had all heard good things about navy rum, and in the event it lived up to its reputation; thick and strong, it lit a fire in our bellies and put us to sleep in short order.

One of the pleasant duties each morning was the egg and milk run to a farm on the other side of the Loch. I usually drove the Austin utility van, taking along a couple of the men who happened to be at a loose end.

At the farm we were treated like sons, being fed milk warm from the cow, and as many oatcakes as we could eat. For half an hour or so we sat contentedly in front of the old lady's peat fire until we felt that Sergeant Houlker would be getting agitated.

Our cook *extraordinaire* was still with us, for which good fortune we were grateful. The rations were extremely good and, supplemented as they were by eggs, milk, and oatcakes, we were living like fighting cocks. All this, and the bracing air, meant we became as fit as any Stradivarius.

No-one knew how long this more or less Elysian existence would continue, so we resolved to make the most of the agreeable conditions while they lasted.

There were three NCOs on the establishment; Sergeant Houlker, a bombardier given to delusions of grandeur, and a lance bombardier, a clerkly, bespectacled soldier who tended to give the impression of a vicar who has unwittingly found himself in the local bordello. Sergeant Houlker ran the shop with great good humour. He was the only sergeant I knew who could issue dire threats with a broad grin on his face.

Unfortunately the bombardier shared our sleeping quarters, where he made a name for himself. After lights out, the lads usually went on yarning in the darkness, until one night when the bombardier abruptly sat up in his bed, clapped his hands like a nanny and called out, 'Now then, now then. It's after lights out. Get to sleep and stop all this chattering.'

When this idiocy first occurred we were nonplussed.

'Where are we,' someone asked loudly, 'in the Army or a bloody

NEW PASTURES

nursery?' He was then told that another word and he would be put on a charge.

The Adjutant surprised and alarmed me one day when he informed me that, with immediate effect, I was to take up the duties of duty NCO and guard commander (unpaid of course). I felt most unsuited to being a commander of anything or anybody, and the prospect of giving orders dismayed me.

The news filtered through to the rest of the lads who found it all rather amusing, threatening to disrupt the guard mounting procedure at the first opportunity. As it happened it fell to my lot to mount guard that very night. I got the grinning men lined up eventually, and as I went along the line supposedly inspecting their turn-out, each man pulled a face. My relief on dismissing them was profound.

None of us on parade had any idea that the proceedings had been watched by Sergeant Houlker. Directly I had dismissed the men, Houlker emerged from his quarters and immediately ordered the men to fall in again. They were puzzled, but not for long. He proceeded to give them a tongue lashing, before giving me a mini-lecture. 'Don't let them bugger you about' was the essence. 'If they try it on, put 'em on a bloody charge.' But I knew the men so well. We were mates, forever acting the goat together. No way could I have put any of them on a charge. They were better behaved on subsequent guard mountings though!

Generally we all got on well. The only exception being one Gunner Bell, known to all as 'old ding dong'. He had served as a stoker in the Royal Navy during the 1914 war, and obviously he was getting on a bit. Short and stocky, with a neck like a bull, and a temper to match, he sometimes erupted violently at some real or imagined slight. We put it down to his naval past, and the fact that he was batman to Major Marshall. Kindred spirits we felt.

On occasion the long winter nights were enlivened by a spectacular show, courtesy of the aurora borealis, or northern lights. The kaleidoscope, flickering and dancing in multi-coloured splendour, had us gazing open mouthed and silent at the strange phenomenon.

Scapa Flow was extremely well defended against air attack. In the early days, the Luftwaffe had put in several sorties, and there was always the possibility of a heavy raid from their Norwegian airfields. The ack-ack defences, however, were powerful, casting an impenetrable umbrella over the entire anchorage. I think the German flyers took the hint and stayed away, with the exception of one or two nosy reconnaissance planes.

DON'T FORGET TO WRITE

I did in fact get a close up view of one such. I had taken an officer up to a conference somewhere near Marwick Head on the northwest coast, and having a couple of hours to myself, I walked to the top of the spectacular cliffs to watch the guillemots, oyster catchers, kittiwakes et al.

I lay stretched out on a bed of heather and sea thrift gazing down at the frothing sea hundreds of feet below, when the sound of an aircraft made me sit up. It came round from the Brough of Birsay at cliff top height, possibly some few hundreds yard distant.

When I saw the black cross on the fuselage, I immediately ducked. I could clearly see the pilot of the Heinkel, and if his gunner had been alert he could have had me jumping about. Nothing happened though, and in seconds he was out of sight.

When I had satisfied myself that the intruder was not coming back for his pound of flesh, I walked over to the huge granite memorial overlooking the sea. It commemorates the loss of HMS *Hampshire* way back in June 1916. Lord Kitchener, and sadly all hands went down with the cruiser.

The long, dark, windswept nights were enlivened on occasion by a dance in the village hall at Finstown. They tended to be noisy affairs, the bar providing Dutch courage for many lads not versed in the social graces. Most of them fell over before the last waltz, not even having seen the dance floor.

Usually the dance kicked off with commendable decorum, but as the evening progressed, some degeneration set in. If there is anything a half-cut squaddie likes, it's a knees-up, and when the sweating band, comprising accordionist, fiddler, piper and pianist got going with the eightsome reel, then things really started to hot up. Army boots thundered, legs and arms flailed, and the wallflowers propping up the bar, attracted by the commotion, loosely joined in causing great confusion. The noise was like a herd of elephants trumpeting and stampeding to a musical accompaniment. A spectacle that would have unnerved the Royal Scottish Country Dance Society.

At close of play I doubt if anyone could have been accused of sobriety, including the band. We knew the end had arrived when the accordionist slipped off his chair accompanied by a terminal wail from his instrument!

Going on leave, although always a welcome occasion, was something of a trial, especially when the Pentland Firth raged and bashed itself against the cliffs, throwing up enormous gouts of spume.

The old *Earl of Zetland* carried us, in what seemed to be leaps and bounds, from Stromness to Scrabster on the northern tip of Scotland. From here we

NEW PASTURES

Former Regimental HQ

were lorried the short distance to Thurso railway station where the men, some still green from the crossing, fell thankfully into the relative comfort of a compartment.

Sometimes the rail journey to Manchester could take anything up to 24 hours or more. It rather depended upon snags farther south such as air raids and diversions. On these occasions two or three of us would arrange our own particular diversion in the shape of a bottle of rum purchased usually at the Aberdeen stop. There's nothing like it for improving a tedious rail journey.

Our rather cushy existence lasted some nine months or so; a period of, if not bliss, something very like it as far as I was concerned. Perhaps the fact that I had not previously been so far afield had something to do with my euphoria, but whatever the reason, the Islands fascinated me, and I was sorry to learn that the Regiment was shortly to return once more to Mather Avenue barracks in Liverpool.

I did in fact return to the Islands nearly fifty years later; a delightfully nostalgic experience. The old house, albeit somewhat jaded in appearance, still looked out over Loch Kirbister, (although the wooden huts had disappeared) and the farm where we had loitered with our oat cakes and milk appeared to have prospered over the years.

DON'T FORGET TO WRITE

Surely though, it couldn't be almost half a century since I took my first guard mounting, and old 'ding dong' blasphemed in the darkness? But the passage of time meant little as I surveyed what had been a rather draughty home from home, and I hope to brave the Pentland Firth once again, before I become altogether too ancient.

The Regiment finally embarked rather untidily on the Isle of Man steamer *Lady of Man*, or it may have been the *Manxman*, I'm not quite sure. The ship was *en route* from Lerwick in the Shetlands, and had called at Kirkwall to pick us up.

Once aboard, we were confronted with evidence of what had been an extremely rough passage between Lerwick and Kirkwall. A group of RAF personnel, on their way to postings or leave, sported broken arms from being flung about. Fortunately the weather had abated as we headed out of Kirkwall harbour on course for Aberdeen.

Somewhere off the Scottish coast, the ship crept furtively into a remote bay and there hove to. This unscheduled stop brought forth a rash of more uninformed speculation. Rumourmongers held sway for a while, their prognostications varying from engine room mutiny to a surprise invasion of Norway. That certainly would have given the Germans a bit of a laugh.

A brief speech from the captain soon put an end to all the wild rumours, although what he said concentrated our minds rather well.

He informed the assembled troops that this hiatus in our short voyage was due to the presence of what he termed 'uninvited' guests lurking somewhere between ourselves and Aberdeen. This could only mean U-boats, in which case we were unanimous in the view that staying put was rather a good idea, especially as we had no escort of any description. So we settled down to wait and hope that the interfering U-boats would clear off.

Some hours later, under cover of darkness and shrouded in a Scotch mist, we slipped out of our hiding place and resumed course for Aberdeen, reaching that granite town without further incident.

CHAPTER 8

Death of the 71st

In many ways I was sorry to leave the Islands; so much had happened there to broaden my experience. But there would be no more warm milk and oatcakes, no more horizontal rain, and above all, no more wild ceilidhs.

We entrained at Aberdeen, and there was plenty of time to consider, as we rattled along, what the future might have in store for me. The Orkney experience had made me restless, and I felt the need to explore new areas of activity, without having the slightest idea of what they might be.

Mather Avenue had changed not at all since our earlier occupation, but some technical progress was manifest with the arrival of sophisticated control equipment for the searchlights. At long last, it seemed we were about to have radar direction.

Shortly after our return to Liverpool, our Commanding Officer, Lt. Col. F. Howarth relinquished his command due, I believe to indifferent health, and on the 25th May 1942 he was posted to RA Depot Woolwich. We were sorry to lose him. He had, after all played a key role in getting the 71st off the ground.

The new CO, Lt. Col. J. P. Hampson was a well known figure in Salford Territorial Army circles, where he had commanded a local unit for some time. His cheerful roly-poly figure contrasted noticably with the ascetic, spare figure of his predecessor.

It soon became clear that the new CO was a soldiers' man. He had that rare ability to be close to the men without overstepping the mark. A rather odd paradox attending the relationship between officers and other ranks lay in the mens' suspicion and disapproval of any officer who tried too hard to be 'one of the lads'.

Our new CO struck a neat balance and earned great respect from all ranks. He always appeared to be in jovial mood, yet there was never any doubt that anyone foolish enough to let him, or the Regiment down, would have had to do some fast talking.

I very nearly found myself in just such a situation one wet, filthy night, as I stood sentry duty on the main gate. I would have been about halfway through my stint from midnight to two in the morning. Rain lashed down and, contrary to established routine, the previous sentry had omitted to warn me that the CO was still out and about somewhere.

The sentry box was a useful place to be on such a night and, wedged firmly in a corner, I began to doze, notwithstanding my cramped posture.

I woke to find Colonel Hampson addressing me. His chubby face peered at me from a couple of feet away, and I became vaguely aware that I should be doing something about the Colonel's presence. I could immediately think only of presenting arms, which I promptly attempted within the confines of the sentry box. I realised my predicament when the rifle muzzle struck the roof of the box with a dull thud. I hardly think the CO was impressed by all the rattling and crashing going on in the farther reaches of my shelter, but at least he waited until I had simmered down.

By this time I had recovered myself sufficiently to join in the conversation, such as it was. In fact the Colonel was merely remarking upon the foul weather, and generally just being agreeable. He made no mention then, or later, to my being patently asleep on duty. I shall not insult the Colonel's memory by suggesting that he was unaware that I had nodded off; benign he may have been, but daft he certainly was not.

This was a restless period for me. Air raids had fallen of to some extent, and I was aware that boredom was creeping in after the stimulating Orkney experience.

I tried to resolve matters by committing the squaddies' sin of volunteering for a variety of transfers whenever anything vaguely interesting came up on the notice board.

My first attempt was to volunteer for glider pilot training. I put in an application and, after a medical examination, settled down to wait.

Several nail-biting weeks later I was informed that the list was over subscribed, so that was that.

Appetite whetted, I followed this by stupidly applying for transfer to the Commandos. Some weeks later the Adjutant informed me that I had been provisionally accepted. I was unsure whether to be pleased or alarmed by the news. But I needn't have worried. The Commandos finally turned me down because of my lack of infantry training.

Not to be thwarted, I persisted in my daft attempts to get away. When a notice appeared inviting applications from drivers for service in the Middle East I lost no time putting my name in.

My imagination revelled in mental pictures of warm sunshine and drifting white sands lapped by the sapphire waters of the Mediterranean.

DEATH OF THE 71ST

By and large, I felt, it could only be a sharp improvement on Liverpool and the Mersey. This time I was lucky, if it could be so described, and within weeks I received marching orders; a posting to the 104th Light Anti-Aircraft Regiment and a travel warrant to Minehead where, apparently, my new Regiment was stationed preparatory to going overseas.

I had mixed feelings about saying cheerio to my old mates in the Regiment. They were a good lot, and although our contribution to the war effort had been minimal, we had done the job we had been trained for as well as we were able.

What I did not know, and indeed none of us knew, was that the writing was already on the wall for the old 71st. It was to be disbanded, and I suppose I just got away before the final blow fell.

The 71st was shortly despatched to the South Coast where for some time sterling work was done against low flying aircraft. The Lewis guns, old as they were, came into their own; accounting for no less than 12 enemy planes over a period of one month.

One man was killed at Hastings, and several wounded before the Regiment folded. All the men were split up and posted piecemeal to regiments up and down the country. Some of them, (including my old boss Captain, later Major Milns) went over to Normandy.

Colonel Hampson issued a farewell message to the men and women of the 71st. The text is probably indicative of the bond that existed between the CO and his command, and I think it is appropriate to record his message in full:

> *'My Dear Troops,*
>
> *The sudden and calamitous blow that has befallen us with the quick dispersion of troops has not permitted me to say "Cheerio" to you personally, to shake you by the hand and to give you my good wishes for the future.*
>
> *It has been a very great honour to me to have commanded this Regiment for the past ten months, and I must thank you for the excellent support that you have given me. You have responded to my appeals with zest and enthusiasm that could not be excelled. You have certainly "gone to it", and "gone one better" on all occasions — courses — night co-operation — athletics, but proudest feat of all — in action against the enemy. Twelve planes in a month is a very proud record.*
>
> *You must accept your ill fortune with fortitude; with a strong resolve to maintain the spirit of "71" wherever you go, and strive to add lustre to your*

41

new unit. Your goal is "final victory for our most righteous cause". Do not be deviated from it; not even by the disbandment of our grand Regiment — this very bitter blow! You must maintain and strengthen your endeavours for the successful prosecution of this conflict.

My life has been enriched by my command of the 71st — all too brief; I have made a host of new friends, enjoyed your companionship, and been proud at the successful outcome of many of our joint efforts. And now the Regiment dies; my cup of grief overflows but my heart remains strong in the belief that you, like me, will put forward your strongest endeavours to conquer this great disappointment and sustain your maximum efforts until the final victory is won.

Good luck to you in the future. With renewed thanks and a host of very happy memories.

Cheerio — keep smiling,

Yours sincerely,

J. P. Hampson TD Lt. Col.'

Col. Hampson was subsequently posted to command a searchlight battery somewhere in Shropshire.

And so, as the Colonel wrote, a Regiment died. I was glad not to have been with them at that rather sad moment in the Regiment's brief history.

CHAPTER 9

104th LAA Regiment

I managed to wangle a short leave of 48 hours at home before embarking on the long journey that was eventually to take me nearly halfway round the world.

The first leg of this latter day odyssey was a wearisome train journey from Manchester to Minehead in Somerset. Fortunately I had the company of someone from my home town so that the hours passed in reasonable fashion between short catnaps and lengthy speculation on what might be in store for us.

Our train clanked into Minehead in the late afternoon. There we were met by a reception committee made up of two sergeants. They strode up and down the platform bawling out, with singular disregard for security, 'All change for Sidi Barrani — next stop Cairo!'

After the usual preliminaries, checking names and so on, we were loaded into lorries and driven to a complex of beach huts near the charming village of Dunster. The location was almost a duplication of Thurstaston on the Wirral, where 462 Battery had languished not so long ago.

We were surprised to find the camp deserted; not a soul stirred save the reception committee, who quickly hustled us over to the orderly room, where there was more taking of names. Here, surprise, surprise, we were handed fourteen day leave passes and travel warrants, before being driven back to the station to board another train going back to Manchester!

My unheralded return to the bosom of the family was more or less what had happened the night I had been called up. After sombre and final farewells only some 24 hours previously, I was now back to hammer at the front door once again. It was all very confusing and unsettling, but I had absorbed the squaddies' knack of accepting unexpected military benevolence without question. Looking a gift horse in the mouth was something we generally guarded against.

Two weeks passed quickly in a whirl of activity. Then the sobering final day was upon us. I packed my kit, polished boots, and tried some brittle conversation with mother who hovered in the background looking grim.

43

DON'T FORGET TO WRITE

Then, suddenly, it was time to go. I think we all knew that it would be a long time before the son and heir hammered again on the front door.

But sombre thoughts were sidelined for a moment, and once again breezy good-byes were said. Father trotted out his, by now, threadbare line. 'Don't forget — soon as you get settled, drop us a line!' Dear old dad. He had endured the trenches of Flanders as a lad of seventeen and, amid all the forced, cheerful *badinage*, only he was aware of what might be in store for me.

On Monday evening, the 11th of January 1943 I again reported at the camp, where the 104 Light Anti-Aircraft Regiment languished awaiting its embarkation orders.

The new arrivals were taken down a long line of wooden huts, to which we were arbitrarily assigned one at a time.

About halfway along the line, the sergeant pointed to one and, turning to me said brusquely, 'That one's yours' and left me to get on with it. I was about to strike up a friendship that would still be going strong over half a century on.

I dragged my kit through the blackout curtain to come face to face with Bombardier Arthur Walton's detachment. Yorkshireman Arthur was polishing his boots, while one 'Dad' Walker, another Yorkshire lad, was standing on his head reading a book. Others were lying on their 'flea pits' reading or smoking in more conventional fashion.

Clearly I had stumbled upon some remarkable company; a detachment of eccentrics to whom 'Dad' Walker's propensity for reading upside down was accepted as quite the normal thing to do.

One of those to welcome me was Johnny McCourt, known to all as 'Mac'. He was a Geordie, a miner from Seaham Harbour in County Durham. Although Mac was as tough as old boots, he was blessed with a dry, cynical humour and a splendid accent that became less intelligible when he got excited.

Confirmation of my acceptance into this nonconformist detachment came by way of an invitation to join the lads in a raid on the cookhouse. We were forever looking for ways to supplement our rations, and as security appeared to be lax, a raid was laid on to seize any bread that happened to be lying around. The raid was successful, but we were eating surplus mouldy bread for days afterwards.

The next two weeks were taken up preparing the Bofors guns for transportation, using up surplus ammunition, and generally preparing ourselves for departure.

104TH LAA REGIMENT

SS Mooltan

On Wednesday, the 13th of January, we paraded and were treated to a pep talk by the Battery commander.

At about 1430 hours we marched off to the station in full marching order, kit bags over our shoulders, and for the benefit of any enemy watchers, pith helmets were attached prominently to our packs. But then, as all seasoned squaddies know, that did not necessarily mean an awful lot. None of us would have been overly surprised eventually to find ourselves up to the armpits in snow. There was, we usually found, an element of surprise in many orders issued by higher authority.

During a long-winded, wearying journey, there was much stopping and starting, and bets were laid as to our likely embarkation port.

All became clear early the following morning as I stretched my legs in the corridor. I could scarcely believe it. The train had stopped on the bridge over Penny Lane Liverpool. The barracks and my old mates at Mather Avenue were a mere half mile away. There was little doubt now about our destination.

The train pulled in alongside the landing stage, and as we piled out we got our first glimpse of the huge troop ship that was to be home of a kind for the next six or seven weeks.

We sat on our packs awaiting further orders and considered the vast bulk now looming over us. It was the 20,000 ton *Mooltan* a rather ancient P&O vessel that, in the earlier days of the British Raj, had been on the India run. Few of us now gawping at *Mooltan* had seen, let alone sailed, in such an enormous ship.

45

DON'T FORGET TO WRITE

Every man jack now twitched to get on board to sample the delights of shipboard life. After the first few days however, many of the enthusiasts would have given a king's ransom to be put ashore somewhere — anywhere!

After the inevitable long wait, the order to board prompted an excited bustle. Kit was hurriedly assembled and up the gangplank we staggered, emerging in a writhing mass on to what was grandly termed the promenade deck.

We were directed down flight after flight of stairs, hobnailed boots clattering and slipping on the metal plates. Down, ever downwards we went until I began to imagine our accommodation might be in the bilges.

Our mess deck, when eventually we came upon it, was well below the water line. Everywhere one looked there were rows of mess tables with forms on either side to seat a dozen or so men at each table. The ablutions and lavatories were, I suppose, *en suite*, since they were located at the end of the mess deck. Clearance between decks was around 8 feet, so that when hammocks were slung, one had to walk about bent double like Quasimodo.

Kit was everywhere, on the tables, under the tables, and stuffed into any odd corner that could be found.

Gradually the mess deck filled up with swearing men and their equipment. The noise, press of bodies, and mountains of kit, soon lent the deck the appearance of a busy and rather foul Eastern market.

I wondered what on earth it was going to be like day after day, night after night, cooped up in an atmosphere of sweating bodies. I was soon to find out.

Fortunately, smoking on the mess decks was pronounced a heinous crime, otherwise, due to the lack of ventilation down there we would have been in a sorry state.

Hours later, we had to some extent sorted ourselves out. The frenetic activity subsided, giving us an opportunity to take stock and get our bearings or, as frequently happened, get lost in the labyrinthine companion ways.

The unmistakable sound of the gangplank being taken aboard had us out on deck in a rush. The significant business of being cast off from shore was something we did not want to miss. There was an air of finality about the procedure. Sadly, for some of those beaming, excited passengers, theirs would be a one-way ticket.

As *Mooltan* edged away from her berth a solitary figure, presumably a docker, stood watching. Somewhere a tug's siren hooted. The man slowly lifted his cap to us, then turned and walked away.

CHAPTER 10

Convoy WS 26

Mooltan dropped anchor in mid-river and there, to the chagrin of many Liverpudlians on board, she stayed, within clear sight of the Liver Birds, for five days. At least the hold up provided an opportunity to become acquainted with our new quarters. We came upon a brass plaque giving some details of the ship. The fact that she was equipped to carry just over 700 passengers we found rather amusing since, as we shortly discovered, the ship now carried no less than some 4,500 souls.

There was great excitement when, early one morning, *Mooltan* weighed anchor and we were off up the Irish Sea accompanied by two other troopers and a destroyer. Someone standing alongside me, sheltering from a cutting wind said, 'Well, never thought I would ever go on a cruise.' Some cruise it turned out to be!

We arrived in the busy waters of the Clyde on the 21st of January. Merchant ships and naval vessels surrounded us. Presumably this was the convoy assembly point.

There was a good deal of coming and going between the various vessels until the night of the 23rd/24th of January. Then we heard the rattle of the anchor chain and the throb of engines. We were on our way at last.

Ahead, the sky looked threatening as *Mooltan* passed between Rathlin Island to port and the Mull of Kintyre over to starboard.

From the promenade deck we had an impressive view of the rest of our convoy. *Stratheden* carried the Commodore who controlled sixteen other ships, among which were *Arundel Castle*, *Empress of Canada* and *Maloja*; the latter being sister ship of our own *Mooltan*. The impressive escort included two armed merchant cruisers, nine destroyers, two of which were Greek, a Free French sloop, and three corvettes. The venerable old aircraft carrier *Argus* took up station on our starboard quarter.

Shortly after passing Rathlin Island we ran into a severe storm that worsened by the hour. Fortunately I was not bothered by sea-sickness, and at the height of the storm I braced myself at the forward end of the promenade deck, watching with mingled apprehension and wonder, as the *Mooltan*'s prow buried itself with a shuddering thud into a massive wall of

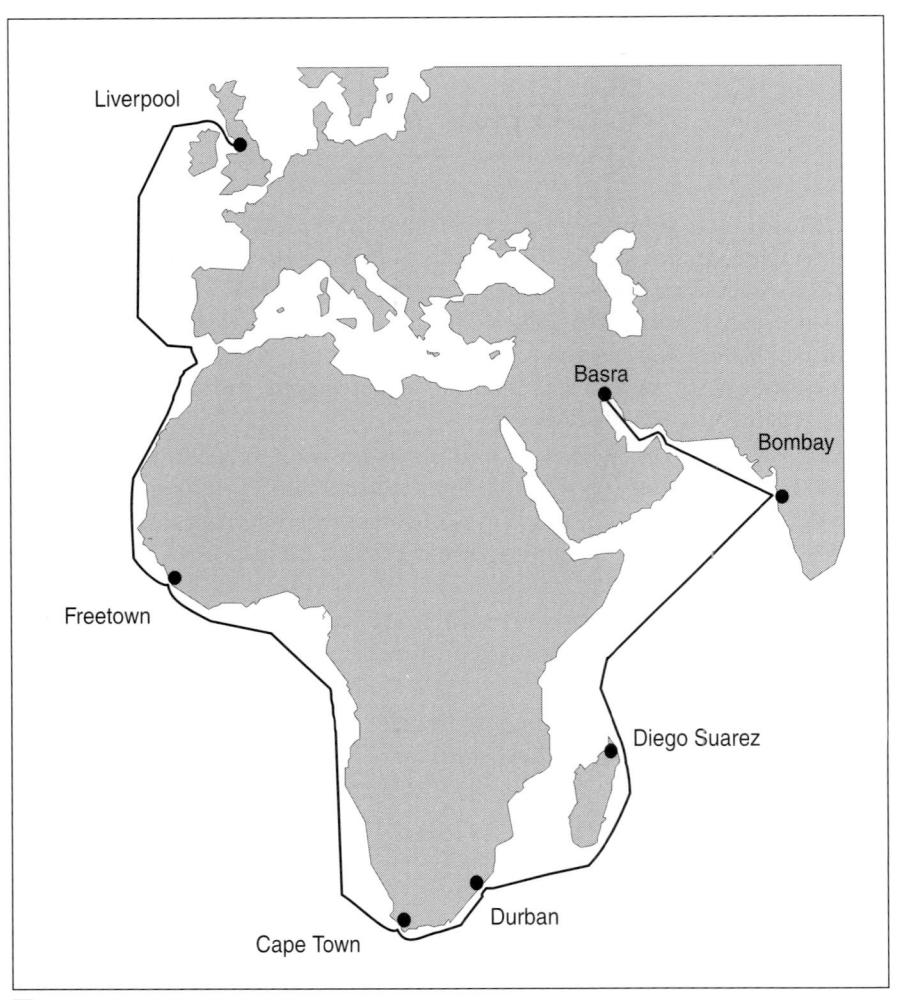

The convoy route

menacing green water. The forepeak remained under the mass of water for what seemed ages. Once or twice I feared the old ship would not recover from the plunge, but slowly she rose from the depths and climbed out of the trough to the crest of yet another massive mast high wave, before plunging down again. It was rather like being on a watery roller-coaster. Each time the ship started its downward plunge the angle caused the screws to lift out of the water, shaking the ship vigorously from stem to stern.

The wind screamed in the halyards, and on the crest of a wave it was possible to glimpse the rest of the convoy through the flying spindrift before sliding down into yet another trough. In those brief moments the ordeal of the destroyers and corvettes was only too plain. What life was like on board those small escort ships could only be guessed at. The crews must have been a tough and tenacious bunch to withstand such a battering, but they stayed with us and we were thankful.

The old *Mooltan* groaned and shuddered, seemingly sharing the general distress, while down below, on the crowded mess decks, men were lying about all over the place in varying degrees of distress. Some lay groaning on the mess tables. Others who couldn't get into the latrines sat just outside the door with their heads in buckets, no doubt praying silently for deliverance from purgatory one way or another.

It was sobering to realise that only a sheet of steel plate was keeping out the thundering waves which struck the ship with such relentless monotony. It sounded like scores of bass drums being struck simultaneously, but I don't think the suffering, groaning men rolling about on the deck were particularly concerned about anything save their personal misery.

I suppose it was inevitable that the 'bogs' (lavatories) would sooner or later become blocked. Water, urine, etc., overflowed on to the mess decks but there was not a lot that the few men still upright could do about it, except to offer sympathy and aid to friends in their wretchedness. The foetid atmosphere down below did nothing to assist their recovery.

Storms notwithstanding, the troops were required to parade on deck at 0830 hours every morning. Not surprisingly the number of men on parade dwindled until, on the third and final day of the storm there were only about half a dozen of us still swaying about answering roll call.

From an entirely selfish point of view, those of us still on our feet benefited from the general malaise in that we scoffed the rations of those laid low. An ill wind certainly, but we stuffed ourselves unashamedly, impervious to the stink of effluent swirling about us.

In the days following the storm, food became an obsession with us all. The rations were meagre enough at the beginning, but as the voyage progressed, the food situation worsened, and our obsession with it.

At mealtimes we took turns to go to the galley with a couple of large dixies. It soon became clear that with hundreds of men bent upon the same purpose, it was necessary to set out on the expedition sometime around mid-morning to join the queue rattling their dixies.

In the vicinity of the galley one was driven to distraction by the aroma of baking bread. But one could only stand there quietly salivating until one's turn came.

No way were we starving, but a perpetual hunger rumbled in our bellies, a condition which inevitably led to some sharp practices.

It was mandatory for all on board at all times to carry his small kapok life-preserver, although I very much doubt if it would have preserved even a cat's life, let alone a fully dressed squaddie. Attached to each of these useless kapok appendages hung a tin about the size of a sardine can containing not sardines but an emergency ration of rock hard chocolate. Those tins, dangling provocatively from lifebelt tapes proved too much of a temptation to the less scrupulous amongst the troops.

Our convivial habit, once darkness had closed over the convoy, was to lean over the rail enjoying a good natter, and watch absently the blobs of fluorescence floating past in the frothing waters below.

Thus engaged, we presented an unmissable opportunity for the silent thief moving about the deck with razor blade at the ready. There was nothing to it. A deft, careful slash, and some unfortunate would find himself minus chocolate.

I found myself in that very situation after one of our chatting sessions at the rail, and during inspection on parade the following morning Captain Saunders, not unreasonably, wanted to know where my emergency ration was. 'I don't know sir,' I said, 'it was stolen last night.' His helpful reply was, 'Then find it before next parade.'

The order left me in no doubt whatsoever. Suffice it to say that on the following morning a tin of chocolate dangled reassuringly from a foreshortened tape on my life preserver!

There was a NAAFI of sorts aboard, whose most sought after commodity was tinned fruit; anything to supplement our rations. The only difficulty again was queuing. It was not unknown for the queue to stretch right round the ship, and after a couple of hours or so standing around one could arrive at the shop just in time to see the shutters go up — quota sold!

An abiding pastime for most of the lads was the inevitable 'Housey-Housey' as it was then known. The school comprised a goodly selection of all the troops aboard, all tightly packed into one of the public rooms. First we were treated to the BBC World Service news broadcast on loudspeakers, heralded, as I believe it is today, by the strains of 'Lily Bolero'. After the news it was 'Eyes down — look in!'

CONVOY WS 26

I tended to regard the game as rather negative until one night, having been persuaded to join in, I got a full card. Unfortunately another squaddie came up with a full house and we were asked if we wanted to split the money or toss for it. I agreed to toss — and lost. After that I gave the whole enterprise a wide berth. I was always a poor loser!

Gradually the atmosphere began to warm up. Ship's officers changed into whites, and we into khaki drill (KD). Then it was sunbathing by numbers. Ten minutes on the back, then turnover for another ten minutes. It was all rather daft, but good fun and plain sailing at last.

Long days passed in weapon training interspersed with turns of duty manning the anti-aircraft guns, and one day the six inch gun on the stern fired off a few practice rounds which shook the old *Mooltan* severely, probably loosening a good few rivets.

Speculation about the possibility of a U-boat attack was fairly constant. We had seen, in our imagination, a gushing wall of sea water overwhelm the mess deck. We knew perfectly well that in the event of a torpedo strike, only a handful of us could hope to survive, but as some wag said, 'Don't worry lads — we're all in the same boat!'

Although the storm had been a misery, it no doubt kept U-boats at bay as we cleared the Western Approaches. But now, in calm waters, we felt exposed and were more than ever thankful for the watchful presence of our escorts.

Lounging at the rail one day enjoying the sun, we watched a Catalina flying boat as it idly circled the convoy. Suddenly it went into a shallow dive. A few seconds after it pulled out, an enormous column of water shot up, followed by a loud boom. More depth charges were dropped, and destroyers quickly detached themselves to join in the hunt. One of them cut across the *Mooltan*'s bows with what seemed only yards to spare.

The commotion lasted for a couple of hours, but there were no casualties. Escorts took up station again and the much maligned life preservers became, even below, constant companions.

At about this time convoy KMF8, including the old *Argus* which had formed part of WS26 was detached, heading away towards Gibraltar and the Med.

On the 6th of February we sighted our first landfall — Freetown, West Africa, described with great relish by several know-alls as the white man's grave. I was not surprised, but in the event we were not allowed ashore, which was perhaps as well; instead we spent an entire evening plastering ourselves with anti-mosquito cream.

Humidity was high. We lay on deck in pools of perspiration, grumbling and praying for a sea breeze.

It was a great relief when, on the 9th, we departed that smelly, sweaty outpost of empire heading south for the Gulf of Guinea and the equator. We crossed the line at 3.15 pm on the 13th of February. The absence of a swimming pool, not to mention chronic overcrowding, meant there was no crossing the line ceremony. However, one of our close acquaintances, Charles, who happened to be a master printer, had made friends with the ship's printer, and together they produced unofficial crossing the line certificates for the selected few. I managed to preserve my copy for many years, but it disappeared presumably during one of our removals.

By this time most of the troops were opting to sleep on deck. Each evening a procession of men appeared carrying blankets to a favoured location, there to spend hours gossiping in the warm darkness. It was a delight to lie on one's blankets gazing up at the sharply sparkling stars, and drop off to sleep with a balmy sea breeze playing over one's face.

Early morning brought chaos. Shouts from the Lascar seamen as they played hoses over the deck had us scrambling to gather up our blankets ahead of the swirling water.

Not everyone was pleased by this noisy incursion on their blissful dreams. The Lascars squirted water with the abandon of demented firemen, shouting, 'Get up Johnny, get up.' Sleepy squaddies replied in obscene terms, adding dubious advice about what the seamen ought to do with their hosepipes. It made no difference though, and one or two heavy sleepers had to scramble off with wet blankets.

Our endless perambulations about the ship often took us past the promenade deck lounge, reserved for officers. They sat at tables draped in starched white linen cloths, elegantly sipping their iced coffee, oblivious to the discontented mutterings from the envious passers-by.

Below decks, hunger had abated somewhat in the heat, displaced now by an everlasting thirst. Occasionally we were treated to an issue of bottled lime juice which, it was alleged, was the army's method of taking the mind off unseemly and intemperate thoughts. I don't think it did a lot of good, apart from slaking an entirely straightforward thirst.

After leaving Freetown, the convoy lumbered off on a south easterly tack taking us deep into the Gulf of Guinea, then we headed south again, keeping fairly close to the African coast.

Meanwhile, after almost a month, we were becoming acclimatised to the fierce brassy sun and the strange, cramped shipboard world. We couldn't wait for our next landfall, wherever that might be. Rations were becoming sparse as the days passed, and even the lime juice petered out eventually.

Thirteen days after leaving Freetown, someone started running about the deck waving his arms wildly and shouting, 'Land — land. Over there!' before disappearing headlong down a companionway.

We looked about us, and there it was — the majestic Table Top mountain overlooking Capetown. Some of the ships were slowly making for the harbour mouth, but *Mooltan* and some other ships had stopped some distance off shore.

It was shortly confirmed that our destination was to be Durban, another two or three days sail round the Cape of Good Hope. There were few grumbles; after all we could manage another couple of days with the promise of bright lights and untold gastronomic delights just waiting to be sampled.

The author and Arthur – Durban beach (with Zulu)

Shortly before we sailed again there was a touching moment when one of our escorting warships, apparently on her way back to home waters, sailed slowly past the line of troopships, its intercom blaring out 'Blaydon Races'. The Captain of the escorting ship stood on the wing of his bridge facing us and saluted each troopship as he passed by. There was a brief moment of silence, then, from thousands of throats rose a cheer that would undoubtedly have been heard in Capetown. It was our noisy tribute to the unceasing vigilance of our escorts on a long and rather dodgy cruise.

Around noon on the 25th of February, *Mooltan* at last eased into Durban harbour. There, on the quayside, stood the now famous 'Lady in White' to welcome us. She was singing 'Land of Hope and Glory' through a megaphone. After some initial embarrassment the troops crowded the starboard rail to join in. This was something totally unexpected, but apparently the good lady was there to greet every troopship to enter Durban harbour. Quite how she acquired advance knowledge of shipping movements we neither knew nor cared. There must be many old sweats still around who remember that stirring greeting from the lady whose name at that time we knew not. In later years her name was revealed as Perla Siedle Gibson. Sadly she has now passed on, there are no more troopships to greet, but she will be remembered with affection by many a squaddie.

There will also be many who can recall the stunning generosity of many other South Africans. As the men trooped thankfully down the gangplank for a brief run ashore, many were whisked off in cars to be fed and entertained in the most lavish fashion.

Unfortunately for us, other ships were quicker off the mark with shore leave, and when we eventually staggered down the gangplank all the cars had gone, leaving us to our own devices. But what the hell — this was Durban South Africa, and it meant food, drink, and bright lights.

There were moments of hilarity as we began to file down the gangplank. Someone started singing 'Fred Karno's Army' to the bewilderment of many native South Africans on the quayside.

Wearing topees for the first time, ancient KD service dress buttoned to the neck, narrow trousers and great clumping army boots, we were straight out of Kipling. Certainly he and Allenby would have recognised us at once. What the locals thought I shudder to think, even today. They may have smiled behind their hands, but wherever we went we were welcomed as if we had just saved them from some sinister visitation.

One evening, as we joined a cinema queue, a lady pushed to the front insisting on paying for the four of us before she returned to her place in the queue. Similar acts of generosity occurred in shops and many forces canteens. We may have looked as if we were just off to relieve Mafeking, but the people of Durban left their mark on us all, and we were grateful for their many kindnesses.

Those halcyon days ended on the 1st of March when *Mooltan* cast off at 0930 hours to join the convoy for the final leg of our voyage.

Our escort now comprised two cruisers, *Birmingham* and *Ceres*, both of which later detached, making for Diego Suarez on the northern tip of Madagascar. We were then joined by the cruiser *Hawkins* to reinforce the six anti-submarine escorts for the remainder of the journey.

Observing the sun, it was obvious that we were heading north, and our amateur navigational efforts were confirmed when we crossed the equator again, this time from south to north. There appeared to be little doubt now that our likely destination would be Bombay. Having experienced a touch of the African continent, we could hardly wait to see what India had to offer us.

CHAPTER 11

Foreign Parts

My recollection of our arrival in Bombay harbour is a jumble of impressions. The Gateway to India shimmered in the oppressive heat as *Mooltan* slid into her berth, and the odours and noise were a far cry from all that we had experienced in Durban. At least we had arrived safely, and now felt thankful that our seafaring days were over, until the Blighty boat of course. But we were wrong — again.

The troops milled about on the quayside in indescribable sweating chaos, stunned by the heat and the hoarse cries of stevedores; choked by swirling dust, and chivvied by NCOs until eventually we were formed up and went marching off into the hurly burly.

None of us had the faintest notion of where we might be going. We could only hope that the officer at the head of the column was reasonably acquainted with his instructions.

The march was fairly brief and soon we were halted on another quayside, facing yet another ship. It was without doubt a most disgusting little tramp ship of Polish nationality. If ever I remembered the name, I certainly couldn't spell it. Someone behind me moaned, 'Christ, we're not sailing on that bloody thing are we?' But we were.

Once again we were directed to the revolting bowels of the ship, where we stood shoulder to sweating shoulder until told to sit down at the mess tables. A sergeant came through and called out, 'Take your shirts off lads, you'll feel better.' They were wet through with sweat and it was a relief to get them off.

After a few minutes, the ship's first officer appeared in the doorway. 'Who told you to take off your shirts?' he demanded to know. 'Get 'em back on again.' We donned the dripping shirts again. A few minutes later the sergeant appeared amongst us again. 'I thought I told you to take off your shirts' he growled, 'Get 'em off like I said.'

At this point there was some mutinous muttering in the ranks. A voice from a dark recess shouted, 'I wish somebody would make up his friggin mind. Shirts off, shirts on — I trained to be a bloody gun layer, not a sodding quick change artist!'

FOREIGN PARTS

The sergeant went away without a word, and the ship's officer found something else to occupy himself with, leaving us to sweat and curse in peace.

We sailed on the 23rd of March in a north westerly direction across the Arabian Sea. The day previous happened to be my 22nd birthday, but I was not overjoyed at having to spend it on a moth-eaten old rust bucket.

The event passed unnoticed and unremarked in a sweltering haze.

What did not escape notice was our fellow voyagers, the cockroaches. They must have outnumbered us by about three to one, and it seemed prudent closely to scrutinise our food. The cook would not have been thanked at that time had he produced 'Spotted Dick' for pudding!

Once through the Gulf of Oman we were into the Persian Gulf heading for the swirling muddy Euphrates and the port of Basra in Iraq, where our odious, nameless ship docked on the 30th of March. We had thus completed 76 days on board ship. This time we appeared to be destined for some soldiering.

There were the usual scenes of chaotic shouting and arm waving before we were marched off to the railway station to be put aboard an uncomfortable train who's coaches boasted slatted wooden seats. At least it was better than walking, and we settled down as best we could. Then we were abruptly ordered off the train. An NCO came round handing out oranges. Speculation was rife as to whether this was a pre-Christmas treat, or just an attempt to keep us going! Someone suggested that the reason for the hand-out was because there was no dining car on the train!

After we had eaten our oranges and darkness had fallen we were ordered back on to the train. It was one thing to get sorted out in daylight, but in the dark it was absolute mayhem. Squaddies trod on each other in their hobnailed boots and cursed in unrestrained enthusiasm. Kit was being thrown into the coaches through the open windows, unmindful of who might be on the receiving end. In such cases the kit was unceremoniously flung back on to the dark platform, much to the annoyance of the squaddie trying to get on board. Somehow we managed to grab a bit of coach to call our own, and shortly, preceded by a strangled, angry bellow from the engine we went jerking and clanking across desert country, our first close up glimpse of desert and camels and palm trees.

No-one, of course, had the slightest idea where we might fetch up. One wag said, 'We'll probably finish up in bloody Baghdad or somewhere like that.' Not that the man had the slightest idea just where Baghdad lay. As things turned out he wasn't wrong.

Group with Mac and Dad Walker

In the darkness at around midnight, the train creaked into a dimly lit station. Our weary eyes could scarcely believe it. A huge sign on the platform; Baghdad, it proclaimed in large roman lettering; and if anyone had any doubts, the name was repeated below in Arabic. By either a superior feat of organisation or pure chance, a fleet of lorries stood outside the station, and in them we were transported to a tented camp on the outskirts of town. This was Quetta camp.

Morning revealed a moonscape of undulating sandy hillocks surrounding the camp. No matter in which direction one looked there was no sign of life, apart, that is, from a large, importunate bird known as a 'Shite Hawk'. The precise origin of that colourful name was never clear to me, but it was a bird given to opportunist thieving. Quite often one of the wretched birds would swoop down upon someone on his way from the cookhouse with two loaded mess tins, to dive at speed and swipe part of the man's dinner. In gastronomic terms this was no great loss, but it was galling to be robbed by a bird.

At Quetta there was no bread for over a week. Instead we were given enormous hard tack biscuits which measured about five inches square by one inch thick. To break them open it was necessary to bash them on a rock. When we looked closely at the biscuits we could see tiny weevils wriggling about. But we ate the biscuits, weevils or no weevils.

By way of a change, we were taken into Baghdad by truck (or passion wagon as it was generally known).

Strangers in a strange town, especially a town like Baghdad, should be chary and vigilant. But we were neither. When this shifty looking Arab invited us in to what appeared to be an interesting and unusual bar, we sauntered in, looking forward to a couple of beers.

It soon became apparent that this was no ordinary bar. We had entered a large courtyard, in the centre of which an elegant fountain played. A first

FOREIGN PARTS

floor balcony ran round three sides, giving access to several doors.

At first we were puzzled. Squaddies were coming and going and we wondered what on earth they were all doing. We were not left in doubt for very long.

Suddenly the door to the courtyard burst open. Whistles shrilled, and in a trice we were surrounded by military police. Realisation dawned rather quickly. This was no bar. We had wandered, innocently enough, into the local bordello, and were very much out of bounds.

Slowly we edged towards the door. Squaddies rushed hither and yon. I saw one shinning up a ladder, trying to escape to the roof. He was trouserless, and his boots, tied by the laces hung round his neck.

At ease in Baghdad

I don't know whether or not he escaped, because at that moment a loud bellow stopped us in our tracks. 'And where the hell do you lot think you're going then?' The voice belonged to the MP major who, presumably, had orchestrated the raid. He glared at us fiercely, but surprised us by accepting our explanation that as it was our first visit to the town, we had somehow lost our bearings. We lost no time in complying with his brusque advice to 'Bugger off then.'

After only a week in camp, recovering from the rigours of an extended cruise, the Commanding Officer in his wisdom, decided we needed toughening up, and the best way to accomplish this would be a route march of some twenty odd miles in FMO (full marching order).

On the appointed day we marched off into the desert. The sun was already well up and threatening. We carried full water bottles but were forbidden to drink from them under pain of severe punishment.

The CO, a sparsely built man, marched at the head of the column. He was not carrying a large heavy pack as the men were, but on the regular pauses he never sat down. On the other hand, the rest of us collapsed in untidy heaps gazing longingly at our water bottles.

DON'T FORGET TO WRITE

I had not even undergone basic infantry training since joining up, and as we plodded along mile after dusty mile, under a molten sun in a temperature of around 110 degrees I felt my legs were about to give way and deposit me in a sweating, exhausted heap in the sand.

Arthur and Mac were marching immediately behind me in the column. They too were weary, but first Arthur, then Mac, relieved me of my rifle. Between them they shared the additional burden until we were almost back at camp. There was no fuss. Neither of them said anything, other than to curse the CO, but left to paddle my own canoe, would no doubt have meant an ignominious end to the march for me.

The column approached the camp gates at last and the order, 'March to attention' floated on the shimmering air. The sentry presented arms and I remember muttering as I passed him, 'What a lucky sod you are mate.'

After being dismissed, it was a blissful lie down with socks peeled off bloody blisters, waiting for treatment by the Medical Officer.

Squaddies, as a general rule, are an undemonstrative lot; Arthur and Mac said nothing about their extra burden on the march, and I don't think I even thanked them properly, if at all. They would only have laughed it off anyway.

Comradeship was a word never bandied about amongst the troops; their sharing of my burden was one of those simple acts of comradeship which made an uncomfortable and often dangerous existence tolerable.

After about a week we struck camp, spending a night under the stars, before being loaded on to lorries at the ungodly hour of 0530 hours. It seemed likely that we were destined to wander the Middle East for ever like some land based 'Flying Dutchman'.

The convoy fetched up in a fly-ridden dust bowl which proved to be Habbanya, an RAF staging post some seven hours or so by road from Baghdad.

The heat here was more oppressive than anything so far experienced, but there was a lake — of sorts. Sunderland flying boats used it and someone said that amongst other things, those Sunderlands were bringing mail from England. This gave us something to think about as there had been no contact with home since the Regiment mustered in early January. It was now mid-April.

The lake, on closer acquaintance, appeared to have the consistency of Mulligatawny soup. It was a relief to immerse oneself in the murky waters, but disconcerting suddenly to see one or two turds floating by. One of the lads said they helped to thicken the soup!

FOREIGN PARTS

The heat was such that several of the lads suffered greatly, and were promptly carted off to the 'cooler' for a few days.

Each morning, the cook and his ack brought round to every tent a large dixie of tea and an equally large dixie of salt water. Before we got any tea we were required to drink a full cup of salt water. Anyone refusing the salt water just did not get any tea.

I must say that after a night lying half buried in sand whipped up by the frequent hot winds, the prospect of greeting the dawn with a mug of salt water revolted most of the troops, but I believe this rough and ready treatment was effective. Today, I suppose, it would be salt tablets.

It was in this God forsaken place that I saw my first mirage. On the shimmering horizon I was surprised to see a huddle of white painted houses surrounded by palm trees. Below the trees, an inviting pool of blue water glinted in the sun. I turned to point out this Shangri-La to someone, but when I looked back it had disappeared. There was nothing to see but broken rocky desert.

Flies in their thousands tormented us from dawn to dusk, intent upon the sweat of our bodies. And one dare not leave a desert sore uncovered for a moment, otherwise it would be black with flies within seconds. At meal times it was necessary to bolt one's food whilst constantly trying to waft away the incredibly persistent intruders.

They followed the food to the mouth, and great care had to be exercised to avoid eating the flies as well.

The fact that we managed to get by without contracting some unspeakable disease could only be due to the many painful injections we received.

Whilst at Habbanya I suffered yet another temporary unpaid promotion, this time to Battery Clerk. It was a cushy number, all to do with parade states and ration indents. the usual incumbent was paid for three stripes, but as far as I could see, there was nothing there to tax the old grey matter; it was money for old rope.

The only good thing to happen at Habbanya was the arrival of the first batch of mail since leaving England.

We crowded in excited anticipation around the mail orderly, ears straining to catch the names being called out. It was a moment to gladden many hearts. All the recipients retired immediately to their tents clutching their flimsy air mails and blessing the Sunderland flying boat skippers. I went off with about eight letters, and for a long time the tent was silent save for the rustle of paper and occasional satisfied grunts.

DON'T FORGET TO WRITE

A month or so later, on the 17th of May, we were up at 'sparrowfart' again; 0430 hours to be precise. After roll call we were put on board open trucks, each seating ten men, all of whom carried their treasured canvas water containers. The convoy moved off in a more or less westerly direction. This time we were told that our destination was Haifa, and to get there we had to cross the Syrian desert.

Our convoy covered something over a hundred boring, dusty miles each day, following the oil pipeline between Haifa and the Iraqi oil fields. At night we laagered at intermediate pumping stations where we slept under the spectacular stars.

The evening chill descended upon us the moment the remorseless sun lowered itself below the horizon. We shivered through the night and soon learned to cover our blankets with gas capes to catch the dew. It was remarkable how much water had collected in the hollows by daybreak.

I have always detested early rising, a condition not helped by our peregrination across the Syrian desert. On three consecutive mornings reveille was at 0315 hours, and on the fourth day we were up at 0245 hours for the final drag into Haifa at around 1300 hours. Now we could see where all that oil ended up. The vast storage tanks must have held hundreds of thousands of gallons, and it required little imagination to foresee the result of a bombing raid. Maybe then, as an anti-aircraft regiment, we were here to join the air defences. But no, I should have known better. They, the faceless ones, the operational planners, hadn't finished with us yet. Within hours we were being herded on to another ramshackle train, bound for God knew where.

The nightmare journey was enlivened to some extent by importuning Arabs. They materialised out of the dark desert night to flog eggs, oranges, and some unspeakable sticky gunge that probably should have been a form of local cake.

As the train squealed to a halt with boring regularity, the vendors in flapping white 'nightshirts' rushed up and down outside like demented spirits, bawling incomprehensibly. Those who had nothing to sell contented themselves trying to thieve kit bags, or any other item of equipment they could get their sticky fingers on.

I woke stiff and creaky after an uncomfortable night, and gazed sleepily out of the carriage window. On the eastern horizon the dull grey sky began to lighten to a pearly grey streaked with delicate tints of mauve, then, on the far horizon, a sudden blaze of scarlet announced a new day. I looked round

FOREIGN PARTS

at the others. Some were waking and stretching cramped limbs, faces painted pink by the quickly rising sun. In the far distance a laden camel loped wearily behind its owner, both indifferent to the clanking train.

The sun was well up when a station appeared out of the sandy wastes. A large decrepit sign indicated our arrival at El Gaza. Everybody off the train, stretching and grunting, relieved to be able to stroll about. Here we breakfasted on jam, bread and tea, before rattling off once again in a southerly direction.

Some hours later we arrived grimy, perspiring and hungry, at El Kantara, another dusty Egyptian outpost, where a meal of Machonachie awaited us. My father used to tell me they were fed this strange concoction during the first war, prompting me to wonder if some of the tins were left overs from 1918. It mattered not. The aroma from those bubbling, steaming vats of stew had us by the throat. No-one raised any queries, they were too busy feeding their faces.

We came to rest finally at a tented camp at Tel el Kebir, in the Bitter Lakes area at the head of the Gulf of Suez. It was here that I again committed the cardinal sin of volunteering my services. The call was for men to train as wireless operators. I knew nothing about radio operating, but I had been vaguely interested in the subject from my early teens. I was keen to have a go and lost no time putting in my name. As things transpired, I never subsequently had cause to regret the move.

Much of our time there was spent on gun drill, parades, kit inspection, FFIs and swatting the ubiquitous flies. When not on duty, Shafto's cinema became a favoured haunt. This establishment was housed in a ramshackle building covered with a rotting canvas roof. For a very few ackers we could take a peek at another world. Sometimes it was a very brief peek due to the film's propensity to break, usually three or four times during a performance. When this happened, the hundreds of thwarted squaddies began a rhythmic thumping of boots on the floor, shouting obscenities at the hapless Egyptian operator. When, eventually, the film came on again, it did so to a thunderous cheer much, I imagine, to the relief of the operator cowering behind his geriatric machine.

Halfway through one of our excursions to never-never land, an enormous desert moon raised itself directly over the screen. There was a great hole in the canvas roof, through which the dazzling silver light shone, right into our faces, completely obliterating the screen.

There were noisy cries of, 'Hey, Abdul, for Christ's sake put that bloody light out!'

DON'T FORGET TO WRITE

The pox doctor's clerks

FOREIGN PARTS

Perhaps the most unpleasant feature of life in those sandy wastes was the Khamsin, a hot ferocious wind which swept down upon us about once each week. They were a severe trial.

A particularly nasty one caught me as I made my way back to my tent holding a mess tin in each hand. I had just collected my meal from the cookhouse and spotted the mass of swirling brown sand tearing towards me. I hurried as best I could, losing most of the tea, but the cloud of gritty choking sand caught me in the open. I felt that my face and legs were being sand blasted.

Inside the tent was a fog of dust. The mess tins contained more sand than food, so I threw the lot out in disgust. But the wind continued to howl, rocking the tent from side to side until finally it collapsed about my ears. I could do nothing but sit there enveloped in dusty canvas and curse.

Someone got to hear of an Arab tailor nearby who could make up natty khaki drill uniforms for a mere pittance. What is more, he could have the uniforms ready in a matter of 24 hours. In fact, some of the lads were already sporting their new gear, and it looked pretty good.

Arthur, Mac, and I ran to earth the wizard of needle and thread in a tent a short distance away. He sat, or rather squatted, before an ancient, arthritic sewing machine, surrounded by bolts of KD cloth of good quality. A solitary oil lamp hung from the roof of the tent, casting a smoky yellow light over the busy scene.

The tailor gazed at us over steel rimmed spectacles, nodded and waved towards a roll of cloth which his assistant thrust under our noses. There followed a degree of haggling, resulting in our being measured up by the assistant. By the following evening our new uniforms were ready. We swaggered back to camp looking, the sergeant major said, like pox doctor's clerks!

Some three weeks later, the 104th packed its many bags, and at 0400 hours on the 16th of June, only three weeks after arrival at Tel el Kebir, we were on the road again wandering, like motorised Bedouin, back tracking over the route of our recent rail journey, over what is now the infamous Gaza strip.

One month after leaving, we were back — in Haifa!

Greatly to the surprise of all, we now became operational — at long last. The guns were deployed around the town and we put in some intensive training. It was all a pleasant change from wandering the inhospitable desert day after thirsty day.

Much of my time was taken up trying desperately to take in the Morse code and elementary facts about the mechanics of a variety of radio sets.

After a week or so grappling with the code in steamy corners, I and one or two other tyros were packed off to the army radio school in Cairo, where we got to grips with the more esoteric facts of radio life.

It was great fun, swanning about in wireless trucks in the lush Fayoum area south of Cairo during the day, and sampling the bars in the city most evenings.

On a more sober note, a gramophone recital at Mena camp one warm evening confirmed my blossoming interest in music. After a tentative flirtation, my enthusiasm for classical music was developing apace, and the recital that evening fired my imagination and opened up for me a completely new and absorbing chapter.

The programme on that occasion was Rimsky Korsakov's *Sheherezade*. Both ends of the marquee were open, revealing a glimpse of the Sphinx and the Great Pyramid of Cheops silhouetted against a rising yellow moon.

In that Pharaonic setting *Sheherezade* had us all completely spellbound. I don't think there was a man there who failed to see the provocative, scantily clad figure spinning her yarns to the old sultan. It was an intoxicating, unforgettable experience.

Before the course ended we were despatched on a lengthy 24 hour exercise. Each wireless truck with its complement of three operators went off into the desert to separate map references given over the air *en route*. At the end of the day, a map reference for the rendezvous point would be transmitted. As the instructor curtly pointed out, 'If you miss that transmission lads — you're buggered!'

His words rang in my ears as the sun set and simultaneously the battery power failed. There was no way now that we could hope to receive that vital map reference. It seemed that we were well and truly 'buggered' as the man said.

Anxious and aimless, we drove over the dark desert, scanning an empty horizon for any sign of life. Shortly we drove into a small village and were immediately surrounded by a horde of locals whose sole interest lay in getting hold of our equipment. Enquiries about the name of the village went unheeded. Men and women crowded the truck. A dozen or so hands fought to get a hold of anything lying about. The situation looked decidedly unhealthy until Norman, who was in the back of the truck with me, grabbed a rifle and pointedly rattled the bolt. That had a salutary effect and the thieving bunch slowly backed off looking affronted.

FOREIGN PARTS

We sped out of that anonymous village like rats up a drainpipe, stopping only when we were well clear to do some more horizon scanning. Charlie, our driver, spotted it first; a dull flickering glow in the far distance. At last! That was surely the rest of the gang. Charlie put his foot down and we went bumping and clattering over scattered rocks in the general direction of the fire.

They were all as relieved to see us as we were them. In fact they made a bit of a fuss, plying us with food and drink as if we had been lost in the burning desert for weeks.

We heard later that our instructor had called for a powerful signals net to put out our call sign and the map reference in the hope that we might just pick it up. Their concern was all quite gratifying and of course we made the most of it!

Final exams brought us more or less to heel. Somehow or other I managed a pass, surprising myself and the instructor.

On the last evening we got together in a bar to celebrate our passes. It turned out to be rather a monumental binge principally on Irish whisky, which did us no good at all. The morning after remains vivid in my memory, but I suppose a good time was had by all.

I returned to my Regiment by train, and at one of its frequent stops we were besieged by Arab children clamouring for baksheesh and food. One ragged little girl of about seven or eight trotted barefoot to my window. It was saddening to see that her left arm had at some time been amputated. She gazed up at me, holding out her good arm, and mumbled something in Arabic. The beautiful dark eyes never left me for a moment. There was no hint of defiance, just a resigned shrug of the shoulder, then she smiled up at me as the train started to move. She trotted along keeping pace, tiny shoeless brown feet raising puffs of sand. She smiled again. I could see anxiety and resignation in her look. I leaned out of the window and quickly handed down a packet of sandwiches I had with me for the journey. She stood by the track, smiling and waving until the train rounded a bend.

Perhaps she would go and sit in the shade to enjoy my butties, and I hoped the others would leave her in peace and not pinch the food. But I would never know. She springs to mind occasionally, and I like to think of her as my little Sheherezade.

Shortly after my return to camp we were off again. On the 16th of July we moved up the coast to Beirut. Our stay in that elegant, sensuous city lasted ten days before we moved farther north to Tripoli. We had not been in that dusty town for more than a day before rioting broke out. None of us knew what it was all about, but we let them get it out of their system before returning to Beirut on the 11th of August.

Any serviceman fortunate enough to have served in that city will, I'm sure, agree that for sheer hedonism few, if any, Middle Eastern cities could match it. There must be many who watched its descent into thuggery and slaughter with great sadness. But we were many years away from all that ghastly business.

We happily wandered the warm jasmine scented streets, exploring the bars. A beer here, and a beer there, until by chance we encountered the Kit Kat Club.

It seemed a likely looking place for a beer and a bit of a sit down.

The entrance was gloomy after the bright sunlight. We had just begun to ascend a flight of stone steps when an exuberant whoop of delight was followed by a white clad female figure sliding at speed down the bannister rail. She took the steps two at a time and shot past us shouting, 'Come on Johnny. You want a beer? Yes, come on Johnny. Come and have a beer!'

A door at the head of the stairs opened on to a large room containing a number of battered settees. In the centre stood a large table upon which were several bottles. The girl in white, who had greeted us with such enthusiasm, dispensed drinks and occasionally, for no apparent reason, performed a cartwheel around the table.

There were several doors leading off the room, and as we sipped our drinks, moving aside now and then to give the cartwheeling girl room, it became obvious, from all the comings and goings, that we had done it again. The girl in white finished her act by leaping on to the table and standing on her head. At that point it seemed as good a time to leave as any.

Our Troop HQ was situated a mile or so north of Beirut, the guns being perched on top of an adjacent cliff overlooking the sea. The location was convenient for the short tram ride into town, a service of which we took advantage as often as possible. We also, I fear, took advantage of the conductor when he came round for the fares. We solemnly assured him that Churchill would pay — an assurance always readily accepted without question.

In course of time we were treated to an inspection by the Brigadier. There were the usual demented preparations. White washing, polishing and tidying was duly supervised by the Troop CO Captain Saunders. Following close on the Captain's heels was his second in command, Lt. Poyser. He, in

FOREIGN PARTS

turn, was followed by the Troop Sergeant Major whose name, thankfully, has been erased from my memory.

This triumvir went poking about the camp intent upon finding something likely to cause displeasure, or worse, to the Brigadier.

Captain Saunders wore his usual pained expression, whilst his second in command tentatively prodded various items of equipment with his cane as though expecting something nasty to leap out and bite. The burly figure of our TSM trailed along at the rear, bullet head jerking from side to side, snapping and barking like a mad dog in a fairground at anyone his beady eye fell upon.

I happened to be on gun sentry duty when the Brigadier and his entourage arrived, welcomed by a welter of salutes.

As some men had found to their cost, the Brigadier insisted, not unreasonably in the circumstances, that all his anti-aircraft personnel should be adept at identifying aircraft. This was not one of my favourite subjects because I was never any good at it. By the time I had identified any aircraft it would have become at dot on the horizon. In any case, I felt that my new occupation with radio meant that it was no longer my business to worry about what we might be shooting at. Let those clever dicks, the gun layers, worry about that.

I nevertheless had a sneaking feeling that the Brigadier would not share my views on the finer points of demarcation, and so put in some quiet study which, in the end, proved unnecessary.

The entourage disappeared into a tent amid a further outbreak of salutes, just as the field telephone in the gun pit jangled. It was control, warning all ack-ack units that a lone, friendly Airspeed Oxford would shortly appear flying north to south, and not to molest it.

I heard the aircraft after a few minutes and trained my binoculars on it. I did not, however, hear the Brigadier's entry into the gun pit. As I turned round he pointed his cane at the rapidly disappearing plane. 'Now' he growled, 'what was that aircraft Gunner?' I could barely conceal a smirk as I replied, 'Airspeed Oxford sir.' If the Brigadier was taken aback, Captain Saunders was dumbfounded. Clearly he could not believe that I, of all the Troop, had identified an aircraft so readily; moreover an aircraft that was so seldom seen around in those days. Our illustrious Captain grinned sheepishly as the Brigadier turned to him, observing, 'Bloody good bit of spotting there Saunders.' Then he waved his cane at me. 'Well done Gunner — well done, keep it up!' I returned to quartering the sky grinning from ear to ear.

69

DON'T FORGET TO WRITE

My relationship with the Morse code was tested to the full when I was despatched to a gloomy building in the city. There I was to assist Royal Signals' personnel in operating a radio link with the RAF on Cyprus. Their job was to flash us a warning of enemy aircraft heading our way.

As usual, it was an all night job which had me falling asleep until roused by insistent bleeping in my head phones. It was often a test call, and I was soon nodding off again.

One warm, sticky night, manning the land line to control and trying not to fall asleep, I stood up to walk off my drowsiness and abruptly keeled over. My legs wobbled and appeared not to belong to me. My head was full of strange noises and I felt sick.

Presumably I was carted off to the MO, because my next awareness was of lying in a supremely comfortable bed, between cool white sheets, and a charming nurse was taking my pulse. I was informed that I had collected a severe dose of sandfly fever and was now languishing in Beirut military hospital. Fever notwithstanding, it was all a pleasant change from the hot tents, flies, and sand encrusted blankets.

My bed was in a ground floor ward. Deep windows looked out on to a cool green garden with bougainvillea and hibiscus lining a shady path. I lay in my spotless bed, rather weak, but appreciative of the supreme comfort. Well starched nurses came to check my pulse, bringing the odd potion for me to drink, followed by far better food than I had become accustomed to.

Gradually, as the fever subsided, I wondered for how long I might hold on to this rather sybaritic existence. I felt no urge to return to the 104th. As far as I was concerned, they could forget all about me.

My mates had other ideas. Arthur, Mac, and Dad Walker breezed into the ward one day to see how I was getting along. Dad Walker was concerned about how well I looked.

'I had,' he said, 'expected to find you nearer death's door than this. It's time you were getting back. You're only skiving.' 'Malingering,' Mac said. 'that's what it is, swinging the lead.' It went on in this fashion until a severe looking nurse padded up and invited them to leave.

Some ten days or so later I was pronounced fit to rejoin the Regiment, where readjustment to life under canvas did not come easily.

The weather was beginning to break and quickly turned wintry, bringing prolonged bouts of rain. Soon we were squelching through sticky red mud. Our boots, cleaned for first parade, were soon caked with the filthy stuff.

FOREIGN PARTS

Christmas was soon upon us and we lost no time getting our feet under the YMCA table. It groaned with goodies, and we were treated to a splendid festive dinner, served by local people who had kindly given their time to help out.

A week or so after Christmas, Arthur and I were strolling past the St. George hotel, a rather elegant watering hole whose clientele included high ranking officers, and no doubt a smattering of James Bonds. Strangely, for such an up-market hostelry, other ranks were not excluded from its hallowed portals.

On occasion, we had entertained the outlandish idea of treating ourselves to dinner there one evening. There was always the possibility of course that we might get ourselves thrown out, but it was a hazard we were prepared to accept. As rumours shortly began to circulate about yet another move, Arthur and I decided to put the matter to the test, particularly as we had a few ackers to spare just then. It was now, or probably never.

Mounting the long flight of steps to the entrance was an ordeal. With every step we anticipated an irate bellow from some, as yet unseen, flunkey. Nothing happened though, and in a trice we were through the door, making a nervous beeline for the bar.

On our left, perched on a bar stool, sat a French naval officer dripping in gold braid, and to our right a full colonel and major conversed in low tones. We probably looked quite shifty as we sidled up to the bar, but the oily haired barman took our orders without blinking. As the drinks arrived, the naval officer waved to the barman indicating that the drinks were on him. He grinned at us and we raised our glasses to him. You could have knocked us both flat with the lightest of feathers.

As we entered the dining room, the *maître d'* greeted us. Well, at least he accepted us into his domain with commendable insouciance. I will admit his eyebrows shot up rather, but we were escorted to a table with some dignity.

Surrounded as we were by a sea of top brass, our early anxiety was nevertheless soon dispelled. No-one looked askance at our appearance. On the contrary, one or two red tabbed colonels nodded to us as we edged timorously past their tables.

The menu was in French, and perhaps the orders were a trifle odd, but we got through the meal in the manner of those born to high living.

One aspect of that outlandish excursion has puzzled me over the years. We went into that dining room without having a clue as to what the cost might be, but we must have had enough of the folding stuff to get by. Just how close it was, I cannot now recall, and perhaps it's just as well.

CHAPTER 12

Italy

Four days after our excursion to the St. George, the Regiment packed its bags, and on the 22nd of January we were off on our travels yet again.

Surprisingly we found ourselves heading south once more, to the land of the Pharaos, finally coming to rest, if that is the word, in Port Said.

Clearly we were about to board ship, although our destination was buried in the profoundest secrecy. Some hopefuls, hard up for a titillating rumour, suggested that we were heading back to Blighty. Some hope. Even the top brass could not have blundered to that extent.

We hung about on the quayside all day, but the moment darkness fell, that was the signal for the chaos to start. Quite why all our moves were executed in pitch blackness we never understood. No self-respecting spy would have given us a second glance.

There was the usual prolonged spasm of shouting and cursing before we were taken out on lighters to board a ship lying at anchor. It proved to be the *Strathmore*.

This was our third ship in just over a year and we were beginning to get the hang of things by then. The demented activity simmered down fairly quickly, then we paraded for roll call as the ship weighed anchor and slipped out of the darkened harbour.

On the 10th of April at 2130 hours *Strathmore* passed through the Straits of Messina. Any doubts about our destination were dispelled at once. Italy's toe looked distinctly uninviting, and I can't say we were impressed when the ship finally edged into her berth in Naples harbour. The battered town had an air of desolation and decay; not really surprising considering its quite recent history.

The Regiment disembarked, forming up on the quayside to await transport for Caserta. We sat on packs and kit bags until late afternoon but no transport turned up. A long walk loomed.

Sure enough, orders were issued to pick up all our personal gear, along with Bren guns, ammunition, cooking equipment, the lot. My personal load was FMO (full marching order), Thompson sub-machine gun and ammunition, Bren gun and kit bag. Thus encumbered we staggered off and were promptly stoned by local youths from behind a wire fence. Surprised and affronted, we assumed they were just expressing anger as a result of their elders having cocked up the war for them, or perhaps they just did not like the look of us — and who can blame them. Whatever the reason, there was no shortage of comment in the ranks. The locals hurled rocks, we hurled abuse, most of which referred to their parentage.

The road climbed steeply from the harbour and, loaded as we were, the march was getting us all down. There was wet tar in places that dragged painfully at the heel of our boots, giving rise to much cursing.

Suddenly, halfway up the hill, some clown of a sergeant, who carried nothing more weighty than a pack, started shouting, 'Left, right, left. Pick up the step.'

The cry was taken up by other NCOs, and before long they were all at it. We human donkeys could scarcely believe what we were hearing. It was as if we were marching on to Horse Guards Parade.

The men were pretty well exhausted, and to have someone bellowing, 'Left, right, left' into their earholes was too much. A man just ahead of me shouted, 'Piss off Sergeant. What the bloody 'ell you take us for — performing bleedin' fleas?' Someone else muttered, 'He must be out of his friggin' mind. If he doesn't shut his face I'll give him a left and right if that's what the bastard wants.'

And in that jolly frame of mind we arrived at the camp site — to find there was no camp, just an open field. 'Well,' we said to each other, 'so what the hell else did we expect. I suppose they'll be telling us next that there's a bloody war on!'

As darkness crept over the field, all the bivvies erected, we flopped down on to our 'flea pits', handed round fags and debated the next move.

It was reasonable to anticipate being sent up to the front line north of Naples. But after a couple of days we were packed into railway cattle trucks for the next phase of our odyssey.

After an interminable wait we departed, amid much clanking and shunting back and forth, in approximately a south easterly direction.

Passing through battered Salerno the train rumbled slowly along towards the Lucanian Appenines. The dark green of olive groves gradually gave way to rolling hills and sparse vegetation. Signs of habitation were few, apart from an occasional lonely huddle of farm buildings.

There were occasions when the train, belching black smoke as it ground away on an uphill gradient, slowed to a crawl, prompting some of the men

ITALY

to drop to the permanent way and stroll along, easily keeping pace with the train.

That journey across the Basilicata was perhaps less wearisome than many of our earlier peregrinations had been. It was a relief nevertheless to hear, at the end of a long day, that we were at last nearing our destination, Taranto, Mussolini's former naval base.

The usual commotion attending detraining and mounting lorries had by this time become second nature to us. At least the lorries were waiting, and soon we were speeding off in convoy to the small town of San Vito. There we were installed in extensive school buildings.

We were unaware as we settled in, but this quiet little Italian town was to be the last resting place of the 104th LAA Regiment.

Taking stock, we found San Vito to be a rather sleepy town, typical of Southern Italy. There was little to excite the lads in that remote little town, and life became rather boring. We had carted our guns around a substantial part of the Middle East in some discomfort, but had not yet fired a shot in anger since leaving England.

The situation brightened a little for Arthur, Mac, and myself when a little wizened Italian one day engaged us in what could loosely be described as conversation. Since none of our triumvir spoke Italian, and he no English, allied to the fact that we were suspicious of his intentions, the *conversatzione* was somewhat fraught.

We worked it out eventually, in the timeless manner of the Englishman abroad by shouting at the poor man and waving our arms about. The upshot, after we had all simmered down, revealed the fact that he was simply trying to invite us to his humble cottage.

This was an interesting development and, although we were unaware at the time, he happened to have two rather pretty daughters; an unlooked for bonus.

Those two virtuous ladies were guarded with a vigilance appropriate to the protection of the crown jewels back home. Hanky-panky, which of course was far from our minds, was quite out of the question.

On our many visits we took chocolate whenever we had any, and the family's delight on such occasions was rewarding. Once or twice though, when we arrived *sans* chocolate, the old man could be heard whispering to his wife, 'Niente chocolate?'

We pretended not to have heard the plaintive whisper, but we felt it wasn't done to winge under the nose of the gift horse. So we decided to regale him with spurious and harrowing stories of the day's bombing raids on Genoa, where lived one of his distant relatives. His usual reaction to our rather theatrical boomings was to throw up his arms, roll his watery eyes, and intone endless and fervent 'mamma mia's' It wasn't very nice of us, but at least it took his mind off chocolate!

At the end of April the billets buzzed with excitement. The Regiment was to be inspected by the Commander in Chief on the 7th of May. None of us had yet seen General Alexander in person, and although top brass inspections were to be avoided like the plague, a rumour was going the rounds that something was up, and whatever that something was would be made known on the parade.

Something was 'up' alright. Alex dropped the bombshell in a short speech following the inspection. The 104th LAA Regiment was to be disbanded within weeks.

It was difficult to accept the fact that the conclusion of all our wanderings about the Middle East was to be the ignominious end of our Regiment. Not even tested in battle, the majority of the lads were to be scattered piecemeal amongst the hard pressed infantry battalions.

The background to this decision was the withdrawal from Italy of divisions and equipment to reinforce landings in the south of France and elsewhere. The 8th Army's operations in Italy, where so many good men had been lost, were to be relegated to little more than a sideshow.

Our guns were taken from us on the 17th of May. And so another regiment died.

During the ensuing couple of idle weeks there was much speculation about where we were all likely to find ourselves in the immediate future. We were not kept waiting for long.

I joined the crush around the battery notice board where the postings had just appeared, fearful about what I might find. Arthur and Mac, predictably, were earmarked for the Infantry Training Unit. Their early army days had been spent with the South Staffordshire Regiment, so their posting was perhaps to be expected.

Alongside my name was the 77th (Highland) Field Regiment who operated 25 pounder field howitzers for a living.

This posting was rather a relief. Notwithstanding my crazy efforts to join such stalwarts as the Commandos etc. I had no particular wish to find myself eyeball to eyeball with some rough Panzer Grenadier waving a Schmeisser at me. I suppose I was getting older and wiser.

ITALY

We made what we could of the brief interlude before dispersal. There were some riotous evenings in a local bar, putting away quantities of vino as if there were no tomorrow. Sadly, for some, there were not to be many more.

Excursions to the town were usually followed by a visit to the cookhouse. It was closed of course, but quite often tea chests that had earlier contained bread were left outside. Always hungry, the three of us spent some time rooting about at the bottom of the boxes, hoping to come up with a crust or two. In this we were often successful. The odd bits of bread helped soak up the vino, but it was hell on the gums!

A mere five days after the postings were published, lorries arrived to take most of the men away to their various depots. Arthur and Mac were amongst them.

From that chilly January evening when I had first made their acquaintance, our friendship had developed apace. Only conflicting duties succeeded in occasionally separating us. Now that the moment had come to say goodbye, one could only think of the many hilarious situations we had revelled in together. We had laughed, cursed, and fretted together, but now it was a round of handshakes and back slapping, with promises to write as soon as we were settled. (Shades of dear old dad in '39!)

Squaddies are not noted for expressions of affection, God forbid, but there was a good deal of forced laughter that day.

Then, suddenly, it was time to go. The lorries started up and they were off, sweeping in a dusty convoy through the gates.

I was never to see Mac again.

CHAPTER 13

The Sharp End

My turn to leave came the following day, when I was taken by lorry to a RA depot up north.

My new Regiment, I understood, was in the line with the 4th British Infantry Division somewhere in the hills north of Cassino. But there was no such thing as arranged transport. It was soon made clear to me that getting to my new home was entirely my own responsibility.

After a good deal of importuning, I managed to cadge a lift with a Canadian transport unit. I was the only passenger, bouncing about in the back like a pea in a tin can.

The route took us over narrow mountain roads, skirting deep tree covered ravines. Perhaps to enliven the journey and relieve boredom, the driver amused himself, and scared the hell out of me, by ramming the rear of the vehicle in front whenever he could get close enough. Hair-raising stuff, but it took my mind off the fact that I would shortly be at the sharp end.

The memorable journey ended when I was deposited at 'B' echelon of the 77th situated in a sparsely wooded area some distance behind the gun positions. There I was informed that my destination was 'C' Troop where I would take over as replacement wireless operator. I should like to have asked what had happened to my predecessor, but on reflection decided that I didn't really want to know.

The ration truck taking me up to the gun position bounced along over a rutted dusty track, and as we rounded the shoulder of a hill we passed under the muzzles of four 25 pounder field guns. These, I was soon to learn, were the pride of my new regiment, and the scourge of many hapless Germans caught on the receiving end of a 'stonk'.

I deposited my kit outside a vacant bivvy and was immediately taken in hand by a rather elderly gunner who was known to all as 'Pop'. A true cockney, he gave me the low down on the personalities, and what to expect. 'Stick to me son' he said, his ruddy face beaming. 'I'll see you right, nuffin to worry about. Gets a bit rough sometimes, but just keep yer 'ead down — you'll be alright sonny.' Then he took me over to the command post to report to the Troop duty officer.

THE SHARP END

No sooner had I arrived than the signaller reported a target from the OP (observation post). The Troop Officer bellowed 'Take post' and in seconds the gunners were standing behind their guns waiting for the order to load.

I was fascinated by the slick procedure. One gunner rammed a shell into the breech with his fist and a split second later another gunner slammed in the brass cartridge case containing the different coloured bags of gun cotton. That last man had to be slippy to get his hand away before the number two slammed the breech shut.

No. 1 gun fired with an almighty crash and away went the first ranging shot. The gun bucked and immediately the breech was flung open ejecting the cartridge case with a loud clang. Within a few seconds the gun was re-loaded and another ranging shot was on its way.

The ranging shots must have registered and soon all four guns were hard at it, the muzzles spitting flame as the layers hit their firing lever.

All this activity was quite fascinating and completely new to me, but helped by Pop's guidance I soon came to comprehend the strange orders and procedures, and to learn something about my Regiment.

I was pleased to find that I was again amongst 'Terriers'. The Regiment had been formed in Glasgow, and after preliminary service with 1st Army in North Africa had been transferred to 8th Army, 4th British Infantry Division, in support of the 6th Battalion, the Black Watch.

Scottish gunners supporting Scottish infantry; couldn't be bad.

The Battalion often passed through our gun lines on their way to take over forward positions. Always they were led by a huge pipe major, and the sound of the 'Black Bear' as they approached never failed to stir the drop of Scottish blood in my veins.

One thing I could never understand was the manner in which those lads greeted us as they passed through. I thought they would have been envious of our position some thousand yards behind the front line. But no. On the contrary they tended to say, 'Rather you than me mate!'

And as they marched along there was always good natured *badinage* flying about, and a few pats on the back from the gunners.

Perhaps the reason for their attitude was to some extent due to their having seen at close hand the devastation wrought when the 24 guns of the Regiment put down a 'stonk'. They also knew that we were often the recipients of some fierce counter-battery fire from the other side.

I soon learned that the strong ties between the Black Watch and the 77th were borne largely out of the former's trust in our ability to put down immediate and effective gunfire just yards to their front if they were being attacked in force. Accuracy and speed were essential in response to any call for assistance, and the men of the Black Watch knew we could be relied upon for speedy action. We, in turn, had a great regard for the 'Auld Forty Twa' as they were universally known.

A Territorial unit ours certainly was, but the prevailing enthusiasm and sheer all round professionalism would have taken some beating.

We took a beating ourselves on my first night. I was sorting out my belongings when I heard a whining noise, followed by a loud hiss and a hell of a bang. This was followed seconds later by another, and what I took to be shrapnel whanging into the surrounding trees.

Pop stuck his head into my bivvy. He looked cheerful enough. 'All right matey? He'll get fed up in a bit — just keep yer 'ead down son.' And having delivered himself of this fatherly advice, retired to his own bivvy.

I was settling down nicely to my new and sometimes disturbing situation when I was earmarked for duty at the OP. An officer, his ack and two wireless operators formed the OP party. The location could be either a hole in the ground up with infantry, or a battered farmhouse from where a watch could be maintained on Jerry activity. Usually we went up in a Bren carrier, a noisy tracked vehicle whose armour plating offered some protection.

Our destination this time was a farmhouse, where we found a large hole in the wall conveniently overlooking the German positions. The officer and his ack settled down to watch whilst Steve Connoly and I established the radio net with the gun position.

There was an awful stink outside from the carcasses of cattle caught in shell fire. It was sad to see the beasts slaughtered in that fashion, but we had other matters to occupy our minds just then.

It wasn't long before we had our first target. We were watching a farmhouse which lay in a shallow valley about 750 yards below us. At first there was no sign of movement until a Jerry Kubelwagon suddenly appeared. Two officers got out of the vehicle and disappeared into the farmhouse.

I passed fire orders to the guns calling for a ranging shot. It came rustling over our heads and landed plumb on the roof of the farmhouse. A flash of flame and bits of timber and roof tiles flew in all directions. The two officers shot out of the house at a run, leapt into the car and tore off at a great rate of knots. A satisfying introduction — and what a ranging shot!

There were fraught occasions though when the OP party was required to be up with the infantry. This meant crawling about in ditches with the

THE SHARP END

gunnery officer and company commander of the infantry; an unhealthy occupation at the best of times.

On one occasion we had taken shelter from a persistent and obstinate Spandau when an infantryman came towards us. His head lay over at an angle, and as he drew level I could see a large lump of shrapnel embedded in his neck. Fortunately the jagged steel had missed his jugular by a fraction. The poor chap seemed quite unconcerned as he ambled along to the regimental aid post. If he was in any pain he gave no indication. In that situation I think I would have been howling.

Since I had learned that the velocity of those razor sharp steel shell fragments travel at around three thousand feet per second, I felt that he was perhaps fortunate that the shrapnel must have been nearly spent when it struck. Closer to the shell burst and he would have been minus his head.

Regular OP duty gave me a sound insight into the miseries our infantrymen suffered as they crouched in their slit trenches.

Constant heavy shelling, mortaring and machine gunning did my nervous system no good at all, and it was always a relief to get back to the guns, although the journey was often a nail-biting exercise.

After a long session at an OP a relief operator came up to give me a break. On the way back in the Bren carrier we found the road blocked by a knocked out Jerry tank, forcing us to go round the back of a blazing farmhouse. Speed was essential. We would be under enemy observation until we regained the road and the shelter of a high banking. Unfortunately the carrier driver proved over anxious to clear the back of the farm. In his haste he shed one of the tracks. We were stuck half on and half off the road in full view of nosy Jerries. Hardly had we stopped than a distant 'bong' heralded a rain of shellfire.

One or two struck the farmhouse, showering us with burning embers and bits of roof tiles. We leapt out of the useless carrier and sprinted across the road to throw ourselves into a ditch. We did not know, nor did we care that the ditch was a mass of barbed wire. We just threw ourselves down, oblivious until later of the lacerating barbs. The shelling lasted about ten minutes and I wondered why the hell the Jerries were making such heavy weather over one clapped out armoured vehicle and two very frightened squaddies. Perhaps some Panzer Grenadier officer was feeling peevish that afternoon. Anyway he did no damage to us or the carrier which was later recovered.

8th Army edged slowly north, and as summer began to fade we closed up to Field Marshall Kesselring's vaunted Gothic Line. Now, anxious to break through before the Germans settled in for the winter, General Alexander re-shuffled his depleted forces. No easy task since he had lost no less than 7 divisions and 70% of his air support all transferred to reinforce invasion troops in France.

The plan for those of us left to carry on was for the Americans to make a feint attack in the mountainous centre of the front, whilst the main push would be made on the right flank, the Adriatic. The plan was code-named OLIVE.

Reorganisation of the front meant the entire 4th Division moving east to new positions as part of 5th Corps on the eastern flank of the Appenines, opposite the German 1st Parachute Division.

A complete division on the move is something to behold and a nightmare for the staff officers. The mountain roads were choked with nose to tail vehicles of every description. Quads towing their guns, supply trucks, tanks, Jeeps, self-propelled guns, wireless trucks and tank recovery units.

The huge crocodile of vehicles eventually came to a halt which lasted for hours. Fortunately enemy aircraft seldom made a nuisance of themselves in those latter days, otherwise the entire division could have been massacred.

We sat in, or on our vehicles with engines switched off and slowly became aware of an uncanny silence. No gunfire of any description disturbed the peace. The silence was such that the inevitable rumours began to fly up and down the column. It was all the result of wishful thinking of course. The Jerries had packed it in. Someone down the line had heard it first hand from a signaller — and so on.

What we did hear first hand some time later was the loud crump of shells falling just short of the road. The enemy had at last cottoned on to the fact that we were up to some mischief. What they did not know however was the fact that the whole of 5th Corps and the Canadian 1st Corps now faced them, ready to pounce.

From our new positions we were treated to a splendid view of the Adriatic. One of our destroyers was sitting off shore about a mile north. She was busy blasting away at enemy positions ashore and getting one or two close ones back. Fortunately she was not hit.

The Greek Brigade, in positions to our front and below us was less fortunate. It took a severe pasting before our Divisional artillery took a hand with heavy supporting fire.

German gunners got their own back later when they gave us a severe thrashing. Shells exploded as they struck the surrounding trees and a

THE SHARP END

number of us leapt cursing into a convenient trench. Minutes later a lorry drew up immediately outside our shelter. The door slammed and the driver, Bert Jones, dropped into the trench beside us. 'Sod this for a game of soldiers' he grunted. 'Buggers nearly had me coming up the track.' He lit a fag. 'What you got in that poxy truck of yours then?' Someone asked. Bert blew out a cloud of Players smoke. 'Ammo' he said with studied nonchalance. We all looked at each other for a moment, then someone in the far corner shouted, 'You daft sod. You gone and parked a lorry full of ammo just outside with all this shit flyin' about? You want to get back in your friggin lorry and piss off somewhere else mate.'

'And you mate,' Bert shouted back, 'can get in my poxy lorry and piss off with it yourself.'

The unseemly and acrimonious debate went back and forth for some time, but Bert crouched in his corner unimpressed by the variety of advice he was getting, and refused to budge.

Summer gave way to autumn, bringing with it prolonged and heavy rainstorms and making life extremely uncomfortable. Underfoot, the dusty roads became sticky quagmires. On several occasions I had to use the Jeep to extricate guns from the mud and drag them to firmer ground.

During one of the many violent thunderstorms my bivvy collapsed wet and cold about my ears. I abandoned the heap of canvas and went in search of alternative shelter until the storm subsided.

The command post on that particular day occupied a section of a deep ditch sandbagged at each end. It had seemed a good position at the time, but no-one realised that they were sitting in a dried up water course. The first indication of trouble was a wall of muddy water as it came boiling down the trench. The first wall of sandbags held the water at bay temporarily, but we had to get the equipment out in a rush. Men who had dug foxholes in the banking also had to get out pretty smartly. Fortunately things were fairly quiet and we were soon able to set up in a less vulnerable spot.

Incoming counter-battery fire proved to be the bane of my life. I was busy servicing the Jeep one afternoon when a loud crack overhead gave me a fright. Shrapnel buzzed past my ear and clanged all over the Jeep. It could only mean that Jerry was ranging on us, and we could expect to be stirred up very shortly.

We did not have long to wait. The gun position came under heavy fire within minutes, prompting a general retirement to our slit trenches.

The bombardment went on well into the night. Then, during a lull, a different bombilation could be heard from the vehicle lines. Several trucks erupted in flames causing pandemonium. Figures scurried about, faintly illumined by the leaping flames. The sudden rattle of small arms fire contributed to the hullabaloo.

After a little while things quietened down and we found that the cause of all the commotion had been a German patrol that had succeeded in penetrating as far as our vehicle lines where they chucked grenades about in some abandon, causing a good deal of damage. It was a skilful and courageous effort.

A letter from Arthur arrived as we slithered and squelched into a new gun position. I sat on the running board of a 15 cwt. to read and re-read it until rain dripping from my steel helmet blurred the writing. Mac was dead; shot by a German sniper when only two or three feet away from Arthur. He bent to lift him, but Mac died within seconds, shot through the head.

It was a long time before I could bring myself to accept that never again would we jokingly complain to Mac about his Geordie accent, and advise him to try speaking English. And now there was a letter to write. But what does one say to a young wife with 5 year old son to care for, and now cruelly bereft of her man?

Staying alive and in one piece was a subject that exercised our minds a good deal, and to this end every man found his own particular stratagem.

One of our young officers was determined to leave no stone unturned, or perhaps more accurately, no chunk of wood undisturbed in his efforts to keep himself intact in every department.

Whenever we took over a new position, that officer's batman was required to dig his slit trench. Not content with a mere hole in the ground, he chivvied his batman, McGregor, to cover the trench with substantial timbers. If, on inspection, the officer found the protection wanting, he would bellow, 'More wood McGregor — more wood.'

Sadly the officer was killed some months later in rather bizarre and tragic circumstances. He was shot by his own troops in Greece. It seemed he had been out in the town and had either ignored the curfew or taken a chance. Either way it was a sad end after all the precautions in Italy.

Forward progress was painfully slow as the Division moved on Forli and Faenza. There seemed always to be another ridge to climb, or another river to cross. And having climbed that ridge and crossed that river, there was yet another one in the distance. I lost count of how many times we were told, 'Just one more hill lads, then the country is flat and the tanks can go in.'

I sometimes thought the officers believed their own fairy tales. What they did not say was that the country north of Rimini although certainly flat, was

THE SHARP END

boggy and unsuitable for extensive deployment of tanks. The fact that some dozen or so river obstacles lay between ourselves and the River Po also appeared to have been omitted from the briefings.

Significantly, one of those rivers, the River Uso, was in fact the historic Rubicon crossed by Julius Ceasar in 49 BC in defiance of the Roman Senate.

The men, however, were singularly unimpressed when this historical fact was made known to them. Their eyes tended to glaze over and you knew they weren't listening. One man said, 'I don't give a bugger who crossed it, just so long as I don't have to.' Fair enough.

Winter was on the doorstep, and as if that were not bad enough I began to be plagued by dysentery. Always the latrines seemed to be in an exposed site, and I don't mean weatherwise. Jerry was apt to be careless about placing his shots catching me in *flagrante* more than once.

My malaise was not improved by being detailed for a recce party one dark, wet night. This meant poking about well forward to try to find a suitable gun position from where we could support the advancing infantry down whose necks we were breathing. The night was full of noise and menace and no-one seemed to know what was going on. We were forced to withdraw after spending part of the night cowering in a slit trench.

Morning came, and with it a new location. No mines had yet been cleared from the area, as was evidenced by a charred body lying beside the track. Evidently the poor chap had been the victim of a mine, which made us extremely cautious about where we put our feet.

Our Troop Officer walked slowly in front of the 15 cwt. truck with eyes down carefully searching the ground ahead. The other operator and I chickened out of riding in the back of the truck, electing to walk behind. If the truck did go up we preferred not to be sitting in it.

The phrase 'walking on eggs' rather sums up the situation. Every footfall was accompanied by a tingling sensation at the back of one's neck, while the stomach churned like a cement mixer. Some of the mines achieved notoriety as 'de-bollickers', so called because they sprang up to waist height before exploding.

Our slow, tentative progress was abruptly halted by a terrific bang and a flash. Bits of the truck shot into the air, but remarkably it did not catch fire. The officer was blown into the ditch but clambered out unhurt. Unfortunately the driver, in spite of the sandbags on the floor of the cab, was in a bad way. One foot was in a mess and he had to be given a shot of morphine before being taken off to hospital.

DON'T FORGET TO WRITE

Some of the mines were cleared by sappers before the guns arrived, but we nevertheless continued to tip-toe about for some time, which perhaps was just as well.

The driver of an armoured half-track on an errand from 'B' echelon chatted to me over a mug of tea outside the cookhouse before getting into his vehicle and driving off. He had gone barely 20 yards before another fearful bang shook us. I looked up to see the front off-side wheel of the half-track go spiralling up in the air accompanied by chunks of stone. I ran to help the driver but found he was unhurt. Shocked and deafened by the blast certainly, but I was pleased to see that the armour plating had protected his feet.

Our brigade by-passed the attractive looking heights of San Marino to our left as we made slow progress towards Forli and Faenza, through olive groves and vine plantations, now sadly neglected.

We came to rest in one such olive grove, and as things were a little quieter, I took myself off for a stroll. Dysentery still tormented me, and I felt the need of a peaceful stroll away, however briefly, from the hurly-burly of the gun site.

I followed a meandering path through gnarled olive trees and was surprised to find a German helmet sitting plumb in the middle of the path. My first thought was to pick it up and carry it triumphantly back to the site.

As I bent to pick up the helmet, alarm bells went off in my head. I got down on my knees and peered under the front of the helmet. Just as well. I could see wiring leading to what obviously was a buried explosive charge.

The thought that I had been but a second or so from being spread all over the Italian countryside brought on another bout of dysentery — hardly surprising given the circumstances!

We ran into a lot of trouble on the outskirts of Forli. My recollections are of a constant barrage of shell fire, mortars, and tracer bullets buzzing past our ears. As one of the old sweats pointed out, in between each glowing tracer there were half a dozen you couldn't see — so, 'Keep yer 'ead down mate!'

As we pushed through the shattered remains of Forli into open country again, my dysentery was getting worse, and for the umpteenth time I reported sick. By this time I was so weakened that I could not stand in the queue outside the MO's hut, I could only sprawl in the dust, shuffling forward from time to time. Maybe I had become somewhat light headed. I recall telling the MO that I was sick and fed up with this constant crapping and would he please give me something to stop it.

THE SHARP END

I rather expected a lecture on how not to speak to medical officers, but he just looked thoughtful for a moment before scribbling something on a pad and instructing me to wait outside.

Since the MO's name was Stott, I suppose in present day parlance I might well have said, 'Bung me up, Stotty!'

Within half an hour I was climbing into the back of an ambulance to join a couple of shell-shocked infantrymen who had been badly knocked about.

Hours later, after a bumpy journey we were admitted to a forward hospital where we got ourselves cleaned up before settling down to a meal and later a comfortable bed.

The following morning I, and a party of other squaddies were taken by ambulance to the quayside at Ancona. There we boarded a gleaming white hospital ship which had a reassuring red cross painted on its sides.

That brief, blissful cruise south to Bari was quite a tonic. An infantryman, a mass of bandages, gazed up at the bridge and said quietly, 'Keep on going mate. Keep going. Just drop us at Southampton, we'll manage from there!'

We were dropped instead on the quayside at Bari.

Nearly all the men had wounds of one kind or another and were taken ashore on stretchers where they were laid in rows.

A medical orderly told me to get on a stretcher. 'Not bloody likely,' I replied. 'I'm walking.' He tended to be argumentative, but in the end he said, 'Well, you bloody walk then mate, but I want you on a stretcher when you get ashore.'

So I obediently lay down on an empty stretcher, feeling rather foolish and something of an imposter. To make matters worse, an RAF aircraftman was going round the prone squaddies lighting cigarettes for them. It was a kindly act, but when he peered down at me I tried to tell him I was fine, and anyway I smoked a pipe. I couldn't convince him, but felt it would be insensitive to tell him to bugger off. Maybe he thought I was shell shocked, and after sticking a lighted cigarette in my mouth, he moved away to minister to a more deserving and receptive case.

The ward sister at Bari military hospital expressed dismay at my emaciated appearance. 'You need building up' she said briskly, and a short time later a nurse presented me with a bowl of hot milk. This became a daily ritual and went down rather well.

Thanks to the medical staff, dysentery soon relaxed its grip on me, and after a couple of rather comfortable weeks being tucked up each night by nursing orderlies, I was despatched to a convalescent camp a few miles away.

DON'T FORGET TO WRITE

There was nothing elaborate about the accommodation in the camp, but it was far superior to winter in the front line, and a change from being shot at from time to time. I resolved therefore to hang on to the camp for as long as possible, and to that end put in some shameful malingering. Although I'm quite certain the doctor was not taken in for a moment, my convalescence continued peacefully.

But it was not to last. A new arrival gave me the exciting news that 4th Division was already being pulled out of the line. They were, he told me, assembling at Taranto for shipment to Palestine.

That did it. If I delayed much longer I should undoubtedly be posted to some other unit still in the line. I wasn't having that. I had to be circumspect, but move with some speed if I wanted to rejoin the 77th.

If the doctor was surprised at my sudden return to excellent health he gave no indication. No doubt he knew exactly what I was up to.

The following day I hit the muddy road and trudged along trying to thumb a lift into Taranto to find my mates. The distance was only some 50 miles but it was a difficult and bitterly cold journey.

Eventually, after a good deal of to-ing and fro-ing, I came upon the unit bivouacked in an open area just outside the town.

I tried the cookhouse for food, then the QM's store for blankets, without success at either. It was made quite clear to me that as I was not yet on the strength, I wasn't really there, and nothing could be done about it. It seemed I would have to remain in administrative limbo until such time as someone recognised my existence.

I was, however, told that I could share Jock McSomething or other's bivvy. This particular Jock was the most objectionable soldier I had ever met. What is more he was an aggressive little man who, I believe, had once been a member of a Glasgow razor gang. His speech was so thick with accent as to be completely unintelligible to a Sassenach, all of which added to the problem of sleeping with him.

The bivvy was designed to accommodate one man and his equipment, so that the immediate prospect of close acquaintance with Jock did not appeal.

I could tell he was no more pleased to see me than I him from the Scottish noises he made, but by that time my blood was up. No food, no blankets, and driving sleet outside. I felt capable of taking a razor to someone myself.

I spent a miserable night shivering in my greatcoat and boots, listening to Jock scratching and farting all night.

THE SHARP END

The following morning I shaved in the remains of a mug of tea, still wearing my greatcoat. Jock was quacking in aggressive tones about something or other. For all I understood he might have been speaking Serbo-Croat, so I ignored him.

Fortunately, after first parade, the QM made up for his intransigence of the previous night, admitting finally that I was in fact there, and awarding me a bivvy and blankets.

Normally parades were boring affairs, but the first parade that morning was an exception.

The Battery Sergeant Major, having stirred us up with a few bellows, gleefully informed the assembly that we were not going to Palestine after all. Faces fell and somebody muttered, 'Christ, we're not going back up there are we?' The BSM heard the plaintive mutter. 'No,' he said, 'we're going some place where you can all play real soldiers. Now listen up. We have a job to do — in Greece. There's a bit of a civil war going on there. Communist guerillas are trying to shoot their way into power against all the democratic principles that many of our mates lost their lives fighting for. So we're going over there to put the silly bastards in their place.' He paused for a moment to let the message sink in, then went into more alarming detail.

We were to be split up into platoons, including specialists such as gun control personnel and wireless ops, taken over there by landing craft, and deposited ashore somewhere near the harbour area at Pireaus.

So the gunners were going to try their hands at being infantrymen — not a pleasing prospect at all. And there was no time for preliminary training we were informed. It was just a matter of getting stuck in and making the best of whatever came up.

The Sergeant Major finished his spiel with the brief sentence, 'And, you lucky lads, we go day after tomorrow.'

CHAPTER 14

Greece

A rear party was detailed to take charge of the guns which were to follow later. Afterwards we were briefed more thoroughly on our new task.

The stark message was that the Greeks, our traditional friends and allies, were starving. Retreating Germans had taken with them horses, food, and anything they could lay hands on. They had also wrecked such primitive agricultural machinery as the Greeks possessed, not to mention the public services which were in ruins.

Our main task was to have been solely humanitarian; to bring what succour we could by the equitable distribution of food, reinstating devastated services, and to provide the basis for reorganising the police force.

The 23rd Armoured Brigade was already in Greece under the command of the extremely able and courageous General Sir Ronald Scobie, a veteran of Tobruk.

Units of the Brigade were spread far and wide, happily in pursuit of their allotted tasks, and revelling in the warm welcome they received. The lads were delighted to be doing something constructive to help our stricken friends.

We had cheered them on in 1940 when they had given the Italian invaders such a bloody nose, very nearly throwing them back from whence they came.

Towards the end of November however, sinister developments threatened to pitch the whole relief programme into the fire.

The two main guerilla forces, EDES (right wing) and ELAS (communist) started to get at each other's throats. EDES was the smaller of the two organisations, and it soon became apparent that ELAS was trying to wipe out EDES in a vicious bid to seize power and take over the government of the country by force of arms.

In furtherance of that aim, ELAS perpetrated the most evil crimes against those fellow Greeks who refused to pay dues to the organisation, or give up the rations our troops had just issued to them.

One ELAS leader known by the code name 'Aris', was responsible for causing the slaughter of ten thousand of his countrymen in the Peloponnese

GREECE

alone, and the dreadful genocide went on, increasing in violence and savagery.

If only ELAS had brought something of that ferocity to bear on the German occupying forces. Instead they took British arms and ammunition dropped to them, and with few exceptions stashed the guns away for eventual use in a bid to saddle Greece with a communist government.

A British liaison officer parachuted into the country had to watch helplessly as German forces escaped northward, while at the same time heavily armed ELAS forces began their march on Athens.

It was established in due course that the rebels had struck an agreement with the Germans to enable each to go their respective ways without molestation.

Every Greek, from the simplest peasant to the professional classes, had reason to fear a visit from those armed thugs. Sometimes it was to drag off a son to serve the cause, or a demand for food and money.

Any civilian of whatever status, rash enough to baulk against the demands were either butchered on the spot, or dragged off into the mountains to be 'interrogated'.

Inevitably British troops became involved when isolated units came under fire from ELAS forces. Bearded rebels poured into towns and villages, attacking police stations, setting fire to the homes of recalcitrant villagers, and generally causing mayhem.

Scobie was incensed. Fortunately, with few exceptions, he was supported by the government at home, and British troops were at last ordered to return fire in self-defence.

The rebels vastly outnumbered the British force, and were able to bring up mortars, heavy machine guns, and even some field artillery. Our positions were attacked in force, and gradually the British pocket of resistance was reduced to something not much more than a square mile, at the centre of which was General Scobie's headquarters.

In response to the General's call for reinforcements, elements of 4th British Division, including our old friends the 6th Battalion Black Watch, were hurriedly despatched to support the hard pressed troops on the Athens perimeter.

Then it was our turn. The 77th now re-cast as an infantry regiment, boarded a Greek tank landing craft in Taranto harbour. This was our first experience of landing craft, and we were unaware of the behaviour of such flat bottomed vessels on the open sea. We soon found out.

DON'T FORGET TO WRITE

Meanwhile, an on-board briefing indicated that our proposed landing had to be outside the harbour as most of it was in rebel hands still. We were advised also that ELAS would probably set about us the moment we got ashore. This information dismayed the troops, and we were rather subdued as our ship nosed into the Ionian Sea.

The lads were even more subdued as we rounded Cape Matapan and headed for the Aegean.

During the night of Christmas Eve the ship started to leap and roll in alarming fashion. Even the Greek sailors were not amused. The fact that the vessel had heeled over during the night, to a point well past the safe angle of roll was only divulged much later, when we had other things to capture our imagination.

On the following day, those who could face it queued at the galley for Christmas dinner. The ship still rolled abominably, and as the galley ran athwartships between port and starboard, one could be staring down through the far door at the boiling, frothing sea one moment then, as the ship rolled the other way, all one could see was an empty blue sky. In the circumstances it was perhaps appropriate that our Christmas dinner comprised hard biscuits and spam. I doubt if any of those unhappy green faces would have relished turkey and plum pudding!

Gradually the weather eased, and soon we had our first glimpse of the Cyclades, grey and olive green below an azure sky. They stood out sharp and clear on the 'wine dark ocean', and as we passed fairly close we could make out a scattering of box like houses, their white-washed walls brilliant in the sun. On a distant hill top a bell tower gleamed blue and white. In those few moments we forgot our tribulations and the torment of an angry sea.

Piraeus finally hove into view, and as the ship edged slowly past a number of obstacles towards our bit of beach, we could hear the rattle of small arms fire and the occasional crump of mortar shells.

All the troops were gathered on deck anxiously waiting for touch down. There was a slight bump, a grating sound, then the massive doors swung open. As the ramp was lowered, a voice from somewhere behind bellowed, 'Hold on to yer wedding tackle lads, we're off.'

We were indeed. Boots clattered on the ramp, and just ahead of me Jock McSomething or other trotted along, carrying on his shoulder a box of ·303 ammunition. Before he cleared the ramp he missed his footing and went over the side, still clutching the box. Some wag shouted, 'Take that man's name — unauthorised bathing!'

92

GREECE

Fortunately the water was only about three feet deep at that point, but Jock's dislike of water was well known. He rose from the murky depths like a particularly odious Neptune, splashing ashore with his box and bawling obscenities as only he could.

Contrary to our information, the landing was without incident, and we waited behind a low concrete wall for our transport to arrive.

As night fell, we boarded a convoy of three tonners for the dash along what the Paras referred to as the mad mile into Athens.

Gurkha troops were just about keeping the road open, but we had to lie flat on the floor of the trucks as ELAS snipers were wont to open fire from nearby buildings on anything that moved.

Our convoy went up the road like the clappers, and as we bumped and swerved, shots could be heard, and one or two pinged off the cab. We managed to get through with nothing worse than a bruising from being thrown about.

The Regiment took over houses in the district of Psychico, a rather posh suburb a couple of miles or so north of the city. My platoon and others settled into a large, attractive house which had an eight foot wall on three sides. (This proved to be of great benefit later.)

A doctor and his wife owned the house. They retreated to the basement area whilst we clumped about on the ground and first floors, to the dismay of the doctor's wife. She was wont to appear, wraithlike, at the head of the cellar stairs to remonstrate with us about noise. But the old dear soon had to put up with a good deal more noise, and all of it lethal.

In anticipation of an assault, window openings were manned, and a slit trench was dug just behind the front garden wall, some 50 feet from the house to accommodate a couple of men and the Bren gun. No-one appeared to have much idea of what to expect, but we were not kept in ignorance for long.

The platoon commander and I shared the trench between 0200 hours and 0400 hours. We were in a commanding position overlooking a fair bit of open ground, beyond which there were several villas, their white walls just distinguishable in the gloom.

Sentry duty was a rather creepy job at that period, as ELAS were known to have killed some of our men with the knife. Until the curfew was imposed, it was often impossible to tell friend from foe since the enemy either wore British battle dress or tatty civvies. For any man standing a lonely sentry duty in the wee small hours, it was rather a skin-tingling time.

DON'T FORGET TO WRITE

Our period of duty was passing very nicely, and there was about half an hour to go when we heard the unmistakable clip-clop of a horse moving about somewhere behind the distant houses. We were mystified. What the hell was a horse doing clumping about at that time of night? Perhaps it had got loose we thought, but the sound persisted until the end of our spell at 0400 hours.

When the relief sentries dropped into our trench we left them to ponder the mystery. All we wanted was a smoke and a catnap before breakfast.

No sooner had we got our heads down than the Bren we had left minutes before opened up with a sharp burst. Almost immediately another Bren sited at the bathroom window joined in. Bullets smacked into the walls, and one or two rounds came through an open ground floor window, showering us with lumps of plaster. Fortunately we were still lying prone on our blankets.

It soon became clear that the invisible horseman was in fact the local ELAS commander who had been moving about organising his men for the attack now developing.

Another Bren, this time from the house occupied by HQ section joined in the racket. They had caught an enemy column marching down the dark road, oblivious to the fact that they were in the sights of a Bren only yards from them. They paid the penalty for not doing a preliminary recce.

Back at the doctor's house it was getting pretty noisy. The gunner at the bathroom window was having a tit for tat duel with an ELAS gunner firing from a window opposite. Our man popped up, fired a burst, then ducked down as the man opposite let fly.

I felt certain that sooner or later the ELAS gunman would break the rhythm by staying put, and waiting for our man to pop up to fire his burst and catch him out. It didn't take long. the double burst from the opposite window just about parted our man's hair. Fortunately he was untouched, but his Scottish ire was roused. He must have emptied two or three magazines into that dark window to the accompaniment of loud oaths. Significantly there was no more firing from there.

Whilst all this mayhem was going on, the troops were not pleased to learn that some newspapers back home, together with a brace of left wing politicians, loudly denigrated our efforts to put an end to the senseless, bloody genocide. The fact that without our intervention, the Greeks would have had a government installed by force of arms appeared not to concern the objectors. They had swallowed whole, the lying propaganda served up

GREECE

Scobie's butchers

by the ELAS leaders, who referred to British troops as 'Scobie's butchers'. We who had seen at first hand, evidence of their butchery of their own countrymen thought this was a bit rich.

America, carried away by an unreasoning antipathy, carped on about incipient colonialism, which of course was utter rubbish. Their press reports were one-sided, and to a large extent re-hashes of ELAS propaganda claptrap, written within the comparative safety and comfort of the Grande Bretagne; in its day, the most luxurious hotel in Athens.

The troops were well aware of such misguided attempts to snatch the rug from under us, but they shrugged it off, usually with the pithy comment that, 'They ought to get off their fat arses and see what's going on in the street', or words to that effect. There was ample evidence of the heavy hand of German and Italian occupation in the pitiful conditions all about us.

Some time later, it dawned on the Americans that had it not been for the prescience of Winston Churchill, and the skill and political awareness of General Scobie, there would have been another communist country to worry about during the cold war, especially having regard to Greece's strategic position in the Mediterranean.

A besetting problem of those days, apart from the obvious one, was the matter of hygiene. Water came on only in fits and starts, depending upon which side happened to be in control of the supply. For the most part it was cut off. The one toilet could not be used, which meant a hazardous trip to the back garden, which, fortunately, was protected by the high wall.

On one such urgent visit I very nearly came to grief. Just as I opened the back door, pausing briefly before throwing myself down the short flight of steps, a bullet smacked into the door frame inches from my left ear. I went down the steps in one bound. Abandoning the venture was quite out of the question! Getting back up the steps took a fraction of a second longer. Another bullet accompanied me, drilling a hole in the door panel. It was all beginning to resemble the Wild West, minus horses or sheriff!

When the section was detailed for a house search, I think we all would have been prepared instead to do the dance of the seven veils in Constitution Square! But there was no getting out of the task. We squatted awkwardly on the outside of an armoured vehicle, all of us armed to the teeth to do battle with ELAS troops who were reported to be holed up in a nearby house.

No-one shot at us though, and after chucking a couple of grenades through the bashed down door, we were inside. A search revealed the body of a very dead ELAS man.

Callously, his comrades had withdrawn, leaving the poor man to bleed to death alone.

Gradually ELAS began to run out of steam. They had expected their march on Athens to be a walkover, but we managed to disabuse them of that notion.

Fighting died down as the rebels gradually withdrew to the mountains on the Albanian border, and soon it was possible to go down to Athens to explore that beautiful city, and enjoy the companionship of fellow squaddies in the NAAFI at the top end of University Street. (Now Zonas, a fashionable meeting place for café society.)

I made a bee line for the Acropolis, and climbed those well worn steps to the Parthenon. At the northern end the Greek flag cracked in a stiff breeze. I was quite alone, gazing out over the russet-hued roofs of the Plaka, beyond which the pointed bulk of Mt. Lycabettus dominated the city.

I treasure the memory of that lonely visit; a prelude to many subsequent visits, when my wife and I gazed out at the enchanting and unchanging view. Sadly, the Acropolis these days is overrun by two legged ants, all hung about with cameras and videos.

GREECE

GOC inspection

The one great bane of my life at that time was the 24 hour guard duty. There was no escaping it, but the next best thing was to go all out for 'stick orderly'. This meant fetching and carrying for the guard commander, and uninterrupted sleep, until it was time to fetch the dixie of morning tea (or 'gunfire' as it was known).

A running battle for stick duty developed between myself and Robbie, a Glasgow schoolteacher. We were good friends, but the competition had a keen edge, and we spent hours polishing and buffing.

On one occasion the orderly officer could not make up his mind which of the two to fall out. He carefully scrutinised the pair of us, going back and forth trying to find something to tip the scales. Then he stood back and pointed to Robbie. As Robbie fell out he smirked at me. At that moment I could have kicked him! Guard duties pursued me to the end, and I never did get the stick orderly's job.

Some months previously, Robbie and I decided that after the day's work, we should bathe, put on clean KD shirts and newly pressed trousers before going for the evening meal. Some of the lads muttered darkly about bullshit. Maybe there was an element of that, but we revelled in being clean and fresh.

The situation in Greece improved gradually and arrangements were put in hand to allow the lads a spot of leave in Corfu. A dozen or so at a time were given passes, and it fell to me to drive them up to Igoumenitsa on the north west coast directly opposite the island. Enterprising sappers there supervised a ferry service, using rather battered infantry landing craft, but the system worked remarkably well.

As we had to pass close to former rebel strongholds it was necessary to go armed, but in the event we were never molested.

A few miles out of Athens the tarmac gave way to dirt roads and potholes. Heavy rains regularly washed away sections of road, especially in the Pindus mountains, so that driving a truck load of men the long distance via Ioannina to the coast was fraught and exhausting. Sometimes I found the rains had washed away all the centre section of road. In fact I once drove with the wheels astride a torrent of water rushing downhill!

It was always a bumpy, lurching and hazardous drive, but the lads, especially on the outward journey, couldn't have cared less. The Corfiotes would welcome them, and all would soon be awash in Retsina or Ouzo.

Before I had an opportunity to visit the island myself, we were on our travels again. This time over the mountains in convoy to Nafpaktos on the north coast of the Gulf of Corinth, almost opposite the port of Patras. There the Regiment settled itself in an olive grove a couple of miles out of town.

In many ways it was a comfortable life; bathing in the Gulf most days, but at least we were now engaged in the job originally intended for the British troops. Officers were doing the rounds of outlying villages, checking on urgently required *matériel* to get farmers and smallholders on their feet again.

Our work for UNRRA, (United Nations Relief and Rehabilitation Authority) was immensely rewarding. The Greek peasants and farmers impressed us all with their quiet dignity. No-one bellyached about not getting enough of this or that. They accepted that we were doing our best in the circumstances. Generally it was a rewarding effort, and I was pleased to have played a small part in it.

One warm day, some of the lads were frolicking about on the beach when someone spotted half a dozen caiques heading for our beach from the general direction of Patras. As each caique beached, it disgorged several young and not so young ladies. Bemused at first by this female invasion, the lads soon realised that those ladies, scenting a profitable afternoon, had brought the bordello to the beach. Even hardened squaddies felt this was a bit much. It's one thing to lurk in a scented, dimly lit room, but an overt performance on the beach was something else again! I should think the

GREECE

ladies returned to Patras somewhat disgruntled.

Army equipment, even in the sticks, was closely guarded, and vehicles especially were not to be left unattended under pain of severe punishment.

I came very close to experiencing that punishment at first hand. I happened to be driving back from Rion and Antirion, a few miles up the coast from Nafpaktos, when I was flagged down by a young Greek woman. Obviously in some distress, she managed to convey to me that her young son was very sick, and she was desperate to get to a *pharmakeion* (chemist) to get some medicine for her boy.

It was all most irregular, but I shot past our camp in a cloud of dust, the woman beside me in the passenger seat. I pulled up in the tiny square and escorted my distraught passenger round a corner to point out the *pharmakeion* to her.

Footloose in Athens

The 15 cwt. I was driving that day was clapped out; if the engine was switched off it was well nigh impossible to start again, so for that brief instant I left the engine running and the vehicle unattended.

No sooner had I turned my back than I heard the engine rev, then the unmistakable sound of it being driven away. I galloped back to the square just in time to see a cloud of blue smoke hanging on the warm air.

I dashed over to a couple of elderly Greeks playing backgammon outside a taverna. They replied to my anxious questions by tapping their shoulders, indicating that an officer had pinched my clapped out vehicle. One of them, familiar with British insignia said simply 'Colonel'. That alarming news convinced me that I would shortly be looking at a prolonged spell in the 'glasshouse'.

Fortunately I was soon picked up by one of the other drivers and taken back to camp. I lost no time in reporting my predicament to the Troop Officer Lt. Pearson.

99

DON'T FORGET TO WRITE

Together we made for the Battery Commander's office to tell him the story before the colonel could get to him.

The major appeared unconcerned however, and the following day I was informed that the CO accepted that in the circumstances I had acted quite properly, and even expressed his approval. So that, thankfully, was that.

The war was drawing to a bitter and bloody close when the Regiment received marching orders for a return to Athens. Those in the ranks unsuited to the calm of rural life were delighted to be returning to the flesh pots. Certainly there was little to excite the troops in sleepy Nafpaktos, apart from the solitary cavernous taverna, and interest in that emporium was beginning to wane.

Nafpaktos is some 300 km from Athens, via most atrocious dirt roads winding over vertiginous mountains.

Often, the road, such as it was, skirted sheer drops of several hundred feet over boulders and rough scree. Those views from the back of a bouncing, lurching lorry, put a stop to ribald songs, and until we reached more stable country, the lads were somewhat tight-lipped.

Although our route took the convoy through Delphi, we were not permitted to stop for a consultation with the Oracle. We did pause briefly to stretch our legs, and watch the eagles as they wheeled round and round, quartering the olive slopes of Mt. Parnassus. Then we were off again, through Arachova, with its huddle of white painted, pantiled houses.

From Arachova it was mostly downhill through Levadia and Thebes, and eventually to join the blessed tarmac road just outside the city. The relief induced by the transition was almost sensual, and raised a mild cheer from the battered passengers.

Shortly after settling down in the city again, in our old billets at Psychico, I happened to be sitting in the Jeep waiting to pick up a couple of our officers, when I spied a familiar figure approaching; it was none other than Captain Saunders of the 104th and whom I had last seen at San Vito. Much to my surprise he greeted me in the manner of an old friend, seemingly delighted to see me again. Not once did he wrinkle his nose in that mildly disapproving manner of those far off Beirut days. In retrospect, I feel we gave him a difficult time one way or another, and I was glad to see that he had survived in one piece.

On the night of the 7/8th of May I sat in a gloomy room whose only illumination was a solitary 60 watt light bulb. My mood, for some forgotten reason, matched the lighting. Someone in another room was listening to the

GREECE

radio. I had just started a letter home when a face appeared at the door; it was one of my fellow operators. 'It's over,' he said, 'finished, finito, kaput. Jerry has packed it in — war's over mate.' And having delivered himself of the momentous news, turned away, quietly closing the door behind him.

And so, the moment we had craved for so long was at last upon us. But there were no whoops of joy, no wild celebratory parties to welcome the peace. Instead an atmosphere of anti-climax pervaded the billets.

Certainly we were all relieved to know that the dreaded Nebelwerfer would never again turn the stomach, nor would the crack of an 88 trouble us. But the lads were to a large extent

Lt. Pearson, Nafpaktos

subdued. Only when the discharge group numbers appeared on the notice board did excitement really take hold.

We were now a peace time army, lethargically buffing up equipment and performing the inevitable guard duties; activities which were becoming acutely boring. I felt it was time to try something different to add a little spice, so, with tongue in cheek, I applied for a transfer to the Intelligence Corps; a move that prompted a rash of caustic comment from some of my acquaintances. My Troop Commander however, whatever his private thoughts, gave me his blessing, and in due course I was summoned to appear before a panel presided over by a red tabbed colonel.

After being questioned thoroughly for about half an hour, I was instructed to wait outside. There I sat twiddling my thumbs for some time before being ushered back to face the panel.

The colonel surprised me by saying that he could offer me a job, but would I be prepared to stay on in the army for a further tour? I was sorely tempted, but the green fields of England and, importantly, my job, not to mention my parents were waiting for me.

101

DON'T FORGET TO WRITE

Soon after the German surrender came the victory parade. Lt. General Scobie, whom the Greeks idolised, the C-in-C Greek forces, and George Papendreou were to take the salute.

An inordinate amount of spitting and polishing preceded our march to Scobie's HQ on University Street, where hundreds of troops assembled to tremendous cheering and clapping from the crowds packing the pavements.

As a precaution against a surprise attack on the parade by our old enemy, a Bren gun was sited on the roof of a building lower down the street. Ted Wilby and I were pleased to be detailed to man the gun. This let us out of the tedious business of endless inspections before the parade.

There was no room on the pavements, so this meant marching together down the wide roadway. No sooner had we set off together than the crowd erupted in a bout of clapping and cheering. It was an acutely embarrassing moment and we were glad when, blushing furiously, we were able to scuttle into the building and man our quiet eyrie. We both agreed that it was better than having rocks or worse thrown at us!

The last of my daft attempts to see if the grass was greener on the other side was behind me, and I was quite unaware that I was to see and smell the green grass of home sooner than I expected.

The Troop Commander climbed into the Jeep one hot day in late August asking to be taken to the officer's club in town. As I drove off he turned and grinned at me. 'Well,' he said, 'you're a lucky chap.' I wondered what he had in mind. 'You'll be pleased to know that you're going home on a month's leave shortly — what do you think about that then?' I was dumfounded and nearly ran into the back of a three tonner. Surely he couldn't be pulling my leg. I asked him when the happy event might be. 'All things being equal,' he replied, '2nd of September — and you're going by air.'

I immediately took up residence on cloud nine and stayed there for a long time.

The prospect of flying did not appeal to me as I had never previously been off the ground, but thoughts of being whisked all the way to England in a matter of hours overcame my worries.

I just had time to write home to give them the news, and have a few drinks with the lads, before I found myself clambering aboard a huge four engined Liberator bomber. This was a nervous moment, but then I reasoned that the crew would be just as anxious to complete the journey safely as the rest of us.

GREECE

Accommodation on board wasn't much to write home about. Two wooden benches fitted in the bomb bay provided seating of a sort for about a dozen or so men on either side, and that was it. Someone remarked, 'I hope the pilot doesn't pull the wrong bloody lever up there. We'd look damn silly, a couple of dozen squaddies being dropped over Italy sitting on a sodding plank!' An air hostess or two would have taken our minds off the chilly discomfort, but we forgave the RAF for their lack of consideration. Just so long as they concentrated on their immediate task and watched what levers they pulled! For our part we sat gazing fixedly at the side of the fuselage, watching the control cables twitching back and forth as we took off, roaring out over the sea on the first leg to Foggia. There we stayed overnight, changing out of KD into warmer battledress.

Early the following morning we took off again on the final leg, heading up the Italian west coast, in the general direction of France.

Shortly after take-off I was treated to a splendid view through a large rear window. We were just passing over the Isle of Elba and it was my first sight of land several thousand feet below, and I wasn't entirely certain that I liked it.

Strict instructions had been handed out as we boarded that under no circumstances were there to be more than one man at a time at the rear of the plane. The rule was enforced for reasons of safety after the earlier loss of a leave plane taking ATS girls home. Apparently the girls had all rushed to that rear window, excited by the view, but thereby upsetting the aircraft's trim. The pilot was unable to recover, not having sufficient height, and sadly the plane went down. The information concentrated our minds wonderfully, to the extent that anyone who stood to stretch was firmly told to, 'Stop rocking the bloody boat mate.' We were taking no chances!

That last leg dragged on for hour after hour. Bored senseless watching the control cables, I tried some arithmetical calculations but concentration was impossible.

Then we all heard the unmistakable thud of the undercarriage being lowered, and there was a change in the engines' tone. We shouted to each other over the din and grinned like children on a day out. Another slight bump and we were rumbling along the tarmac. Home, or near enough, at last.

We disembarked through a circular hatch forward, and as I dropped to the perimeter grass, the smell of English countryside hit me. I could scarcely believe that this was what the countryside always smelt like in late summer.

25 pounder

It was a wonderful welcome to Peterborough, one I shall never forget.

WAAF girls received us with smiles and cups of tea, the first of either since leaving Foggia, then we were swept off in lorries to a nearby transit camp. In each hut were lists of train times to all parts of the country, and comprehensive instructions on how to get about the area.

I wandered off to a phone box down a leafy lane to telegraph home. The hawthorn hedges were rampant with foxglove, cowslip, and burgeoning blackberry. As I reached the box, a land girl rode past on a bicycle. I was no doubt in a state of euphoria, but I saw in that brief moment an illustration of the expression 'English Rose'. She, however, took not the slightest notice of me and pedalled off.

However, the girl on telegrams was kind and helpful, wanting to know where I had been and hoping that I would enjoy my leave. This friendly reception put me in good heart for the run home.

My parents, a favourite aunt, and my much younger sister Pat, were all at the platform to welcome me home. At least they were all there except father, who had gone missing again. He had gone off to check up on something or other. He was forever disappearing to check up on something or other, and to mother's rage, frequently got himself lost in the process.

GREECE

I went in search, and found him loitering by the booking office looking anxious. I would like to say that we embraced, but neither of us was terribly good at that sort of thing. Instead we shook hands rather formally, and grinned happily at each other.

The welcome committee and I piled into the old Morris and, with my kit bag lashed to the bonnet, off we went down the sloping forecourt of what was then London Road station, threading our way homeward through the battered, familiar city.

Father, never one for half measures, had obtained an enormous Union flag which, to my dismay, I saw hanging from my bedroom window as we turned the corner into our street. Observing my embarrassment, mother was quick to assure me that all returning servicemen were greeted in that fashion, and instructed me not to be so po-faced about it.

It was good to be home, re-united once again with all the favourite aunts and uncles, most of whom now crowded noisily into our sitting room. We required no agenda for that meeting. In between eating and drinking it was a matter of fielding a battery of questions and catching up on the whereabouts and activities of half a dozen cousins scattered about in various parts of the world.

I was pleased to discover that serving members of the TA were entitled to petrol coupons when on leave from overseas. The coupons were issued from the TA Association, then in Blackfriars House. I knew the place well, having started work in that imposing building shortly after my fourteenth birthday. I presented myself there without delay, clutching appropriate documentation, and came away triumphantly waving coupons for a few gallons of precious petrol.

The month flew by in a whirl of activity, doing the things I had dreamt of as I lay in the muck of a slit trench. Simple things like sleeping in a warm dry bed, eating from a plate rather than a tin can, having a hot bath, riding on a bus, and the sheer bliss of being able to sleep without being shaken awake in the wee small hours.

I savoured every moment of my good fortune. The month at home had sharpened my senses again after the years of stagnation. Time passed relentlessly, and all too soon we were gathering ourselves for the awkward good-byes. This time a genuine light heartedness prevailed. I would, with a bit of luck, be back in six months or so — this time for good.

Father came to see me off at the station, and as I passed through the ticket barrier he called out to me, as I knew he would, 'Now don't forget to write — let us know you've got back safely.'

DON'T FORGET TO WRITE

I have no doubts as to father's anxiety to hear from me, but his favourite lines, I realised, were father's way of skirting round an emotional moment. He had, I suppose enough on his hands trying to placate mother, who still quietly held father responsible for encouraging me to get mixed up in a war!

I arrived at Peterborough station just in time to miss my connection. The next train was not until 0830 hours the following morning.

The squaddie's first instinct in such circumstances is to cover his back, and to this end reported my predicament at the nearest police station. I had come thus far without blemish; I had no intention of going back escorted by a couple of red-caps.

My next task was to find a bed for the night. I returned hopefully to the station where I had glimpsed a Salvation Army sign.

A chill autumn wind swept along the platform and I was glad to see there was indeed a Salvation Army dormitory there. I was given a comfortable, spotless bed, and the following morning woken in good time for my train.

Amongst service men and women everywhere, the Salvation Army is greatly respected for doing so much to ease the servicemen's lot, often in far away places. It mattered not to those men and women of the Salvation Army whether one was agnostic, atheist, or whatever religion from C of E through to Buddhism; there was always a welcome, a friendly greeting. Even in areas close to the front, they often appeared with their battered vans under all manner of conditions, ready to dish out 'char and wads' (tea and buns). We owe them our gratitude.

On arrival at the airfield I reported, armed with my note from the police, and was given a bed for the night.

We were up again very early in the chill darkness, shaving under the indifferent light of a 40 watt lamp. There followed an equally indifferent breakfast before being assembled in groups for loading on to Lancaster bombers. There were no formal seating arrangements on board so we just squatted on the smooth metal sheeted floor. Until take-off, when the powerful acceleration had us sliding down towards the tail, grabbing at anything handy to avoid finishing up at the tail end. Our minds were much exercised by what had happened to that ill-fated Liberator with the ATS on board.

Somewhere over France I plucked up courage to climb up into the mid-upper gun turret, now minus guns of course. I gazed about me in some awe. There were another half dozen or so Lancasters in formation with us, quite a sight. I wondered if those down below perhaps thought we were off on a

GREECE

bombing mission. I was thankful that at least no-one was shooting at us, otherwise I might have had another attack of dysentery!

After another overnight pause at Foggia we roared off again on the final leg, over Southern Italy and the Ionian Sea. And soon, turning east over the Peloponnese, we began to lose height, eventually sweeping in to the Kalamaki airstrip from seaward at virtually nought feet.

There were no WAAF girls here, smiling or otherwise, and certainly no cups of char before we were loaded on to lorries for a rather smug and triumphant return to our less fortunate comrades back at the Psychico billets.

I was rather surprised to find my bed in the corner was just as I had left it. Two planks of wood supported at each end by empty 'flimsies' (petrol tins), and my three blankets lay folded at the head. I might only have been away for the weekend.

The sergeant in charge of transport, a rather lumpish, unsoldierly figure whom I shall call Freddie, gradually introduced me to odd jobs in his domain, such as checking the petrol stores and generally relieving him of the more mundane administrative work. I minded not at all; we got on well, and being busy brought my demob number that bit nearer. Both of us had become confirmed Greekophiles by then, and he in fact shortly married a charming and dignified Greek lady of some substance.

Freddie was well educated, but a somewhat lugubrious appearance belied a public school background. He was certainly brighter than I, but would have been sadly out of place on a parade ground.

Just before the wedding he ambled over to me. He was frowning, and I could see there was something on his mind. 'Aitch,' he said, (it was always 'Aitch') 'We're going down to Kalamata for our honeymoon — at least that's the idea, but we need a driver. What say you about driving us down there in the Jeep? It's a hell of a long way Aitch, and you know what the roads are like. Be a bit rough, and it will mean going there and back twice in a couple of weeks. Anyway, for the present I have cleared everything with the Battery Commander, so it's rather up to you. Let me know what you think when you've mulled it over.' 'No need,' I replied. 'I can tell you now. I haven't chauffeured a sergeant on his honeymoon before, but you know me, anything to get off guard duty — I'd be glad to do it.' He looked relieved, slapped me on the back and lurched off back to his office.

It would indeed be a long, tiring journey across the Peloponnese, taking in Corinth, Argos, Tripolis, famous Sparta, and finally Kalamata nestling at the head of a wide inlet on the south coast.

DON'T FORGET TO WRITE

I made the Jeep ready for its unusual and possibly fraught journey. There were no garages or petrol stations in those hulking great mountains of course, only military installations which were few and far between. So it seemed prudent to go prepared for the unexpected.

Freddie married his Greek lady in Athens Cathedral. It was a dignified, if lengthy affair, and after a brief reception for a couple of drinks, we quickly loaded the Jeep with the couple's odds and ends of luggage. I was anxious to get as far as possible before darkness fell.

My passengers sat coyly on the back seat, possibly holding hands. Although being bounced up and down on a hard seat was hardly conducive to romantic thoughts.

A calamity I had not envisaged manifested itself in a spasm of backfires accompanied by sparks from the exhaust. We had come a very long way. Darkness was beginning to settle over the mountains as we approached a deep ravine spanned, it appeared, by flimsy looking wooden planks. Freddie and I walked over it tentatively. It looked dangerous in the fading light. The newly weds, we decided, should walk across and I would follow with the Jeep. The timbers creaked ominously. I glanced fearfully over the side, but the bottom of the ravine was lost in a mass of trees and rocks; clearly no place to linger, and in the age it took to reach the other side, I developed rather a muck sweat.

A decade later, I found that the rickety old bridge had been replaced by a concrete affair and driving over it lacked the *frisson* the wooden bridge created.

We moved off again accompanied by a series of disturbing backfires that reverberated about the brooding hills. Sparks shot out of the exhaust, providing a pyrotechnic display, and establishing beyond doubt that we were rather up the creek minus paddle.

When I lifted the bonnet, the problem was all too clear. The battery had broken free of its restraining straps as a result of the battering over the foul roads, and now it was just a disintegrated heap.

The prospect for the honeymooners was looking rather bleak. But just as I slammed the bonnet down, I spotted a string of lights moving down the mountain in our direction. It appeared to be a convoy, and if we were lucky it could be bound for Kalamata. My guess proved correct. It was in fact a Greek army convoy whose drivers treated the ramshackle bridge with disdain, rattling across with apparent unconcern.

Our predicament amused the drivers no end, but we were soon hitched up behind the lead vehicle, to be towed at a brisk pace into town. I left the

GREECE

vehicle in charge of the local gendarmes for the night, and went thankfully to a bed provided by relatives of the bride.

After a rather odd breakfast of something like baklava swimming in honey, I was off on the scrounge. Fortunately there was a small service unit in Kalamata which looked promising, but the sergeant in charge was loth to part with a battery. 'Bloody 'ard to get 'old of,' he grumbled. 'An' it's on my charge too.' I gave him a rambling story which held his attention for a while, but he was acutely suspicious. In the end he gave way, but not before I had signed about half a dozen army forms, and solemnly undertook to bring a replacement back on my next trip in two weeks time.

The following morning I said my goodbyes to my hosts, and rattled away into the hills on my long treck back to Athens. This time I made regular stops to examine the battery housing. I wasn't about to be caught again.

Shortly after his return, Freddie got his demob papers, and the very same day I was summoned to the Battery Commander. He informed me that for the remainder of my service I would henceforth take up the duties of Acting MT Sergeant. Yet another unpaid promotion, but why worry? It meant that for the first time in my army career I was excused guard duties, parades, and all the other irritations we were heir to. I sat in my little office and watched the guard mounting through the window!

Freddie, who was staying on in Greece, had conceived an idea to buy up surplus army three tonners and set up a transport business. Given the parlous state of transport at that time, it could hardly have failed. He did his damnedest to persuade me to join him in the venture, but I felt I had to turn him down. It was tempting, but the scent of the English countryside was still in my memory. The tall hedgerows lining the lanes, and the 'English Rose' got the better of me. I just could not turn my back on all that. Anyway I rather fancied the role of prodigal son!

CHAPTER 15

Blighty

Gradually men disappeared from the billets as their turn for repatriation came up. A lorry load here, a lorry load there, all thinned out the Regiment as the weeks passed. Saying last goodbyes to the lads who, for almost two years, one had lived, laughed, argued, and often cursed was in many ways a doleful affair. Addresses were exchanged amid some forced ribaldry, but it was sobering to know that, as the lorries departed, it was highly unlikely that one would set eyes on them ever again.

It was a particularly uncomfortable moment when we of the 'Fleetwood Follies' finally shook the hand of our mad bombardier. He pranced about in the back of the lorry, shouting demands that we should visit him at Fleetwood. 'Bring a quid or two with you lads, and we'll all have a good piss-up!' Then the lorry rattled away and he was swallowed up in a cloud of dust.

My turn came shortly afterwards. I clambered into the transport with mixed feelings. Those who were left to fill the gaps were youngsters, just as I had been over six years previously; inexperienced and gauche, with a lot to learn. At least their school would be stable and peaceful.

I squeezed on to a wooden seat next to a lad from Ramsbottom. He started to sing an irreverent version of a hymn well known amongst the old soldiers —

> *'No more church parades on Sunday,*
> *No more asking for a pass,*
> *We will tell the sergeant major*
> *to stick his passes...'* etc.

The blasphemy was lost on the lads. In the midst of all the euphoria of having survived, and home sweet home beckoning, I don't believe we gave a thought to the irreverent singing. After all, it was a moment that many thousands of men and women had prayed for day after miserable day. I doubt if the momentary profanity would have troubled Him overmuch. Of more concern to the Almighty must surely have been the millions of souls who had perished in the fight.

BLIGHTY

As we drew away from Psychico for the last time, some Glaswegians rent the air with a rendition of the 'Ball of Kerrymuir'. What the locals made of it all I cannot imagine.

A dismal, tented camp within sight of bustling shipping, became our temporary home for about a week. Then we embarked on one of Henry Kaiser's 'Liberty' ships, bound once again for Naples.

Our arrival in that dusty city was greeted on this occasion by an apparently indifferent populace. No-one threw rocks at us, and we were allowed to make our way to the railway station without let or hindrance.

On route to Milan, we stopped off at a former Fascists' barracks for a few days before entraining for the final run across Switzerland and France.

The marbled elegance of Milan station, the huge concourse, and the expansive, handsome booking office area, were in such contrast to the dusty, grit laden pigeon holes of British stations.

It did seem to be rather a paradox, and gave me something to ponder upon as the train wound its way northward into the craggy, snow covered peaks of Switzerland.

At the border town of Domodossola, the panting steam engine was taken off, and in its stead an electric loco was attached to carry us across Switzerland. The authorities there presumably objected to our leaving a trail of unseemly smoke and soot to sully their manicured fields, or the immaculate cattle grazing there. The latter gave the impression of being well scrubbed.

This time the train boasted padded seating, which made a change from Egyptian railways.

We stopped briefly at Lausanne but, being in uniform, were forbidden to set foot outside the train. Naturally enough this daft order was ignored by most. We were not about to pose a threat to the stability of Switzerland; all we wanted was to breath in the cool, sharp mountain air for a few forbidden moments.

After clinical Switzerland, it was a long rumble through France. Here and there groups of people toiling in the fields paused to give us a wave as we thundered past. Anglophiles almost to a man in those days!

Weary but excited, we rolled into Calais at last. Just one more short hop — famously baulked at by Hitler — and then Blighty. How often, as we beat ineffectively at a million flies, or cowered frightened in a slit trench, had we yearned for this moment. No anti-climax now as the channel ferry thundered the last twenty miles or so in short order.

On the other side, customs became inquisitive when some hopeful tried to get through with a bulging suitcase, and I fear that one or two squaddies were promptly divested of some rich pickings. The rest of us were briefly questioned before being passed through to the London train.

Once there, some of the lads dumped their kit at the station and went off to let the capital know they had arrived. I couldn't be bothered. The prospect of home had me bustling north, impervious to London's doubtful pleasures.

Father and sister Pat, who was now growing up in great style, were at the station to greet me. The rest of the family were at home in noisy conclave waiting to join in the greetings — and that blasted Union flag was hanging out of my bedroom window again!

CHAPTER 16

Last Act

I was formally discharged from military service on the 20th March 1946, entitled to three month's release leave, before being transferred to the army Z Reserve. One more day's service and it would have been a straight seven year stretch exactly. Yet it seemed more like twenty-seven years since Maurice and I had passed through the gaggle of 'groupies' on that March evening in 1939.

Many times I have speculated on my possible fate had we postponed our visit to the barracks for just one week. That Army Council instruction would have beaten the pair of us. Would I then have settled down to wait for conscription? I really don't know, but of one thing I am certain; I would not have liked to miss that comradeship which was so evident in the TA. And that period prior to the outbreak of war, albeit brief, proved to be a useful introduction to army life.

Upon discharge, all squaddies were given individual testimonials from their CO. Mine still brings a smile. 'Military conduct exemplary. Smart, obliging, and hard working. Versatile in a number of jobs.' Well, that last bit was true enough, but perhaps it would have been more appropriate to record — 'Versatile in a number of unpaid jobs!'

In addition to this shining testimonial, the government gave me a gratuity of £70. It doesn't seem much to-day, but in 1946, although certainly not a fortune, it did help one to ease gratefully into civilian life.

I elected to return to my desk after just one month of gadding about. The £70 ran quickly through my fingers as I went about buying decent shirts and underwear, as far as my clothing coupons would allow. And it seemed to me that I ought to abandon this life of Riley and get down to some remunerative work. The fact that marriage was very much in the air spurred me on. I was going to need a good deal of the folding stuff very soon.

Dear old Arthur Barnes, rotund as ever, was glad to have me back at the desk from whence he had despatched me seven years earlier. I too was glad to see him again, not to mention the new salary scales then being paid!

I slotted into civvy street with no problem, believing reasonably that the army had finished with me, and I with it — but I was wrong!

113

DON'T FORGET TO WRITE

Z training at Towyn Camp

One day in 1952, a brown envelope dropped on the mat. It was from the MoD informing me that as a Z Reservist I was required to report to the military camp at Towyn in south west Wales for, the letter said, further training. 'Training for what, for God's sake' I shouted. 'Haven't we all bloody well done enough?' There was no use shouting though. They had me firmly by the short and curlies.

The cause of this bombshell, if that isn't an unfortunate word, was Russia's threatening behaviour; posturing as did Hitler in the thirties.

Our government's response was also reminiscent of that unhappy period. Men and equipment were hurriedly scraped together in a fatuous effort to counter the perceived threat, and I could see no way of dodging this ridiculous recall to arms.

And so it was that I came to say my goodbyes again; this time to my wife Joyce, and nine month old son Philip. Fortunately, provided the Russians behaved themselves, I would be away for only two weeks.

As things turned out, the whole episode was a complete waste of time and money — a complete and expensive sabre rattling farce. None of it would have been necessary however, had the Russian leadership not been so bloody minded.

Father insisted on taking me to the station in the faithful Morris. For a few moments we stood at the ticket barrier talking nonsense to each other until the guard started slamming doors. Father patted me on the shoulder.

LAST ACT

'Right lad. Time to be off I think.' I gave his shoulder a light tap, which was the nearest either of us would get to a display of emotion. And as I passed through the barrier, I heard him call out, 'Now lad — soon as you get down there — don't forget to write!'
